JOHN BERRYMAN

COLUMBIA INTRODUCTIONS TO

TWENTIETH-CENTURY

AMERICAN POETRY

JOHN UNTERECKER, GENERAL EDITOR

JOHN BERRYMAN

AN INTRODUCTION
TO THE POETRY

JOEL CONARROE

COLUMBIA UNIVERSITY PRESS

NEW YORK

1977

Library of Congress Cataloging in Publication Data

Conarroe, Joel, 1934–
    John Berryman: an introduction to the poetry.
    (Columbia introductions to twentieth-century American
poetry)
    Bibliography: p.
    1. Berryman, John, 1914–1972—Criticism and inter-
pretation.   I. Series.
PS3503.E744Z6   811'.5'4   77-8461
ISBN 0-231-03811-9

Columbia University Press
New York—Guildford, Surrey

COLUMBIA INTRODUCTIONS TO

TWENTIETH-CENTURY

AMERICAN POETRY

This book is for Peter and Terry, and for Stephen, David, Alison, and Jennifer, too.

In the evaluation of the dominant moods of any historical period it is important to hold fast to the fact that there are always islands of self-sufficient order—on farms and in castles, in homes, studies, and cloisters—where sensible people manage to live relatively lusty and decent lives: as moral as they can be, as free as they may be, and as masterly as they can be.

Erik Erikson, *Young Man Luther*

Contents

JOHN UNTERECKER

Foreword

A foreword to this study of Berryman is hard to write: partly because Joel Conarroe so brilliantly—in ways John Berryman would, I think, have approved—illuminates Berryman's work and partly because the combination of Berryman and Conarroe is so heady as to turn every reader into an instant collaborator.

What follows is not so much an effort to anticipate the major patterns outlined by Conarroe as to set my own head in order: to let the collaboration that Conarroe and Berryman drew me into finally run its course. It becomes, I believe, an "engagement" of the sort most readers of this book will experience, something on the order of what Martin Buber calls "dialogue," in this instance a secondary consequence of the interaction of Berryman's jaunty and urgent poetry with Conarroe's sensitive and insightful mind.

I think what strikes any reader of Berryman is how very self-conscious an artist he is: he practices a self-conscious craft, he achieves a self-conscious and deliberate range, he is almost arrogantly self-conscious in his use of the personal. He knows precisely what he wants to accomplish and how to accomplish it. He also knows how very much of his material has to be shaped by the dark turbulence of the human psyche, that essentially immature self, that rebel child all of us to our peril discipline or to our peril allow to break free. Out of the insecurities and disorders and disasters of his life, he constructs with mathematical care what may be the most mature poetry of the twentieth century.

Consider, for example, that self-conscious craftsmanship. Berryman's manner, even in the sonnets, is casual: "I prod our English: cough me up a word" (Sonnet 66). Yet the casual is most artfully contrived. For Berryman, who was in love with form, recognized early on that form gains in power as it is tested. Form, order, harmony—the cohering principles—are attractive but in their purest states not necessarily characteristic of high art. The totally harmonious work, pleasant enough, can be and frequently is dull. On the other hand, out of the conflict between form and formlessness, order and disorder, harmony and the inharmonious can come work of extraordinary intensity: the late quartets of Beethoven, the "terrible" sonnets of Hopkins, passages in *Lear*, and almost everything in *The Tempest*. Works of this sort—along with poems by writers as diverse as Wyatt and Hardy and Emily Dickinson—afforded Berryman not models but objects for study. And study taught him that the most effective forms are those that can be forced into flexibility, forms with perimeters elastic enough to provide maximum "stretch," maximum tension.

The job of the artist is to cram into such forms accurate representations of feeling. Under pressure, his works will seem almost—but not quite—to explode. The explosion, when it takes place, is within the consciousness of the audience.

Does this explain the apparently loose design of the *Dream Songs*, most of them three stanzas of six lines each—except when (as in songs 18, 73, 342, and others) Berryman's material demands an extra 'partial' stanza of from one to three lines? Does it explain why most of the stanzas are ticked off in a rhythmical pattern of five beats, five beats, three beats, five beats, five beats, three beats—except when (as in song 286) pressures of sense and feeling seem to alter that structure almost beyond recognition?

Perhaps. But form is more than superficial shape. Schemes of rhythm and rhyme and stanza are what the craftsman struggles against. The opening song (279) of the seventh and last section of the *Dream Songs* gives Berryman a chance to talk about himself as a craftsman: "If ever he had crafted in the past—/ but only if—he swore now to craft better." And he goes out of his way in this very 'regular' song (rhythms, except for a couple of reversed feet, give the illusion of being almost text-book clean; most rhymes chime out with meticulous precision) to demonstrate how very neat he can be.

But the neatness—like the statement of the poem—barely conceals an underlying violence. The year in Ireland that Henry is looking forward to will, he says, be "tense with love." And if we read carefully, we can also see how tense the poem itself is.

The neat end rhymes (dead/bread, East/ceased, books/nooks, past/fast, better/letter, above/love, to cite only the neatest) conceal a much more sophisticated sound system—one made up of a complex pattern of repeated words and edgy partial rhymes.

The first word of the poem, in fact, is linked by concealed rhyme to the last word of the "Henry's Farewell" sequence that ends section VI. In that poem, all of Henry's friends have taken off for "the west" (an echo of the suicide/death theme that dominates the entire book), leaving Henry alone to pack up for his trip to Dublin and "get on toward the sea." Song 279 picks up immediately that *sea*-sound and plays on it through the rest of the poem: "*Lea*ving *be*hind the country of the dead/ where *he* must then *re*turn & die himself/ *he* set his tired face due *E*ast." A battery of *he*s and *the*s (reinforced by a *cea*sed) continue the rhyme to the last line where it is concluded by that whole "*ye*ar" that will be tense with love. A diagram of partial rhymes of this sort, and repeats and near-repeats of individual words (whereto/where/where; one/one; O/O; books/book; letter/letter; slow/slow; crafted/craft; if/if/if; etc.)—all tension builders—would incorporate about a third of the words of the poem.

Multiplication of examples is probably unnecessary, but two instances that combine rhyme and repeated words are worth a moment's consideration—if only to show how well technical craftsmanship supports the thesis of this song: that a year of anticipated peace will, in fact, not bring peace but tensions of work and love.

Henry has just announced that he is leaving America, the country of the dead (all his dead friends, most of them suicides, and his dead father whose suicide so traumatized his childhood). But America is also the land, he says, to which he must return in order to "die himself." He sets his "tired face due East" toward Ireland, where "had paused a little the war for bread/ and the war for status had ceased/ forever." But Henry's own war for bread and status is still going on, as we learn from surrounding dream songs and obliquely from this song itself. Shoulder to shoulder rhymes like *war* and *for* in the lines I've just quoted are, because of their unexpected proximity, immensely powerful though almost inaudible. They make our ears itch, but only after analysis do we know why. But when "war for" is repeated and then followed by a variation ("*war for* bread," "*war for* status," "ceased"/*for*ever"), ears not just itch but ache. A war is set up in our ears that denies the peace Henry claims he is looking forward to. We are well prepared for his final statement that he will be "tense" for a whole year.

An almost identical situation occurs in the echoing rhymes and repeats involving the sound *O* and the word *book:* "he *took* with

him five *books,/* a Whitman and a Purgatori*o* . . ./ an Oxford
Bible with all its bays and *nooks* . . ./ and one other new
book-O"—echoes that continue in the strange assertion that he
expects now to "craft better" but "*only*" if he had indeed "crafted
better in the past" and that the new crafting, if it takes place at
all, will be "*slow, O slow* and fast."

To the extent that the tensions created by these combina-
tions are resolved, they're resolved in an ambiguity in the meaning of the song that so far I've scrupulously avoided—for that has
to do with Berryman's range, the second characteristic that seems
to me to mark his maturity as a writer.

That Berryman has great range and that he worked hard to
achieve it is, as I said before, self-evident. Berryman tackles all
the big subjects: the big emotions (love, friendship, hatred, fear,
passion, anger), the big intellectual concerns (politics, race relations, the value of history, the nature of art), the big spiritual
questions (the 'reality' of a God, the significance of good and evil,
the function of sin and redemption).

Song 279, for all its superficial neatness, tackles a very big
subject—though that big subject seems at first no more
significant than the unobtrusive technical devices that in tense
interaction give the poem much of its strength.

If his strong subject doesn't at first dazzle us, Berryman,
nevertheless, gives us clues enough to suggest that he is dealing
with significant matters. For example, there are the five books
Berryman takes to Ireland with him: a one-volume dictionary, a
Bible, Dante's *Purgatorio,* a Whitman, and a "new book-O"
which is either the late poems of Yeats (Conarroe's candidate) or
the still evolving *Dream Songs* (my candidate) that we learn in
the immediately following songs is unpruned ("four times too
large") but almost finished ("the large book largely done"). What
Berryman hopes we will recognize, I think, is that he has with

him the book of words itself, the book of moral dilemmas, the book that organizes into a system the healing agony of those who must suffer toward salvation (but *not* Dante's book of the damned or his book of the blessed), "the greatest poem so far written by an American" (Whitman's "Song of Myself": see *The Freedom of the Poet*, p. 227), and the book Berryman expects to be his own major work.

But what about that book, a book with as many "bays and nooks and bafflements" as the Bible and one concerned with as many ethical and spiritual and moral excesses as Dante and Whitman combined? Will Berryman finish it at all? *Not necessarily* seems to be the conclusion of this song. Henry swears to craft better than he had in the past, but *only* if he can be persuaded that what he once accomplished was indeed craftsman-like. Also, his new capacity to work hinges, he says, not on him-self but on "Hands above" that may or may not permit work to take place. And yet he immediately insists he *will* work: "I'll work on slow, O slow and fast." Does that mean he'll make haste slowly? Probably. But it might also, of course, mean that he'll work slowly and practice penance (he'll fast). That love that he'll be tense with: will it be eros or agape—a new mistress or the direct love of God? Will the nature of that tense love have some-thing to do with the compulsion to work both "slow and fast," or will it have to do with moral and/or physical abstention (fasting)?

Perhaps it's no accident that these hovering questions lead to a hovering rhythm in the last two lines of the poem. "Art is techni-cal," Berryman wrote in 1965 (*Freedom*, p. 327). Exposing a hov-ering rhythm might help expose some of the mysteries of the poem.

Henry has just dealt with the fact that he's resolved to work, even though he may not end up working and even though the quality of his work will be out of his own hands. Up to this point in the stanza, the rhythm has been regular as clockwork (pentameter, pentameter, trimeter, pentameter). We expect another pentameter and another trimeter, and we can get them by some sing-song scansion:

> if ā | léttēr | cómes Ī | wīll ańs|wēr thāt léttēr   5
> ānd mȳ whóle | yēar wīll bé | tēnse wīth lóve.   3

In fact, however, a more conversational reading produces something considerably different:

> īf ā lét|tēr cómes | Ī wīll ańs|wēr thāt léttēr   4
> ánd mȳ | whōle yéar | wīll bē ténse | wīth lóve.   4

—which totally violates the scheme of the poem. What I think Berryman really hears, however, is a cross between this and something odder and yet more accurate still, something that, had we terms for it, would be scanned this way:

> īf ā lét|tēr cómes | Ī wīll ańs|wēr thāt lét|tēr [weighted pause]   5
> ānd mȳ whóle yéar | wīll bē ténse | wīth lóve.   3

So far as I know there is no technical term for an accented silence or for two short syllables and two long that are treated as a single foot, but I'm pretty sure that this is what Berryman wants us to hear. (It's just possible that, as in my second version, he accents the opening word of the last line and so 'completes' the feminine ending of the line above, but that scansion bothers my ear and I think would hurt his.)

The effect of the special wobble he achieves is to make the poem build dramatically toward the phrase "whole year." By putting so much weight on that phrase, Berryman forces us to examine the nature of wholeness. (Needless to say, *entire* is, in context, the obvious meaning of *whole*. But behind the word *whole* is the rest of this song, a song that is concerned with a man's one-year departure from a land of the dead and his expectation that at the end of the year he will return there to die; with the fact that his preparation for that death will involve acceptances, denials, and commitments; and with the additional fact that the wholeness of the year can be attained only through tense reconciliations of the demands of body and soul.)

Some questions: Does wholeness involve man's effort only (work), God's will (man's crafting subject to the action of "Hands above"), or some intricate combination of the two? Does wholeness involve peace only or peace plus war? Does wholeness involve faith only or faith plus doubt? Does wholeness involve soul only or soul plus body? Does wholeness involve salvation only or salvation plus sin? Does wholeness involve life only (or death only) or the momentary intersection of life and death (dying)?

Elsewhere, Henry volunteers tentative answers to some of these questions. But nowhere does he find the answer to a question that nags at him through the whole book: Where is the mysterious and *empty* "middle ground" that in the last song Henry feels ought to be "between things and the soul" but that in fact isn't there? If unreconciled opposites can ever achieve wholeness, their reconciliation will occur not in space or time but in intangible arenas that, like Henry himself, will necessarily be "tense with love."

Finally, I want to consider Berryman's self-conscious use of personal materials. Like everybody who speaks of Berryman, including Berryman himself, I blur *The Dream Songs'* Henry and his creator. "The poem," Berryman insists in his author's note, ". . . is essentially about an imaginary character (not the poet, not me) named Henry." But Berryman protests far too much for us to take him at his word; and elsewhere (*Freedom,* p. 330) he mentions that in the first song a character called "I," who "disappears into Henry's first and third persons," may "perhaps" be the

" 'I' . . . of the poet." Henry is not Berryman, in other words, but he is 'inhabited' by Berryman. When he writes of other writers, Berryman is far more open about the function of personal material. In an essay on Robert Lowell, he points out, "One thing critics not themselves writers of poetry occasionally forget is that poetry is composed by actual human beings, and tracts of it are very closely about them. When Shakespeare wrote, 'Two loves I have,' reader, he was *not kidding*" (*Freedom*, p. 316). In 1966, writing about John Crowe Ransom, Berryman was even more candid: "I used to take more seriously than I do now the denials and asseverations, including my own, of poets about their work. . . . A certain sly desire to baffle the onrushing critic is nearly standard in poetic temperament" (*Freedom*, p. 279).

Berryman inhabits his characters and—much more important—so do we. Precisely because they are so full of private stuff, they remind us of ourselves. Because Berryman accepts his own stubborn self and *uses* it, Berryman forces us to participate in and to share that self.

In recognizing this paradox—that the unique individual is in fact everyman—Berryman is freed to take liberties that in lesser writers lead to pointlessly 'confessional' writing. But confession—'exposure'—is the last thing Berryman is interested in. Truth, on the other hand, is something that means a great deal to him. By turning the events of his life into significant fictions—by being both himself and his 'other'—he is able to let us also discover truth, not truth about Berryman but truth—to hover on the edge of a dangerous phrase—about our own being and about the nature of being itself.

The risks Berryman takes—all calculated ones—are extraordinary; his accomplishments are those of a master.

Acknowledgments

I want to express my gratitude to Kate Berryman, Dr. and Mrs. Boyd Thomes, Mr. and Mrs. Arthur Naftalin, Lars Mazzola, John Unterecker, Daniel Hoffman, Jay Rogoff, Peter and Terry Conn, Maurice Johnson, Geoffrey Harpham, Philip and Martha Grausman, Philip Roth, M. L. Rosenthal, David Ogden, Cybele Katz, Jeffrey Bottiger, Julie Tonkin, Colleen Davis, Frank Nye, Jeffrey Cain, Robert Storey, Gerald Weales, William Bernhardt, David Diefendorf, Bruce Schimmel, and Alice Lavelle, all of whom provided valuable help of one sort or another during my work on this project. I am much indebted to the Corporation of Yaddo, which kindly invited me to inhabit its peaceful premises during the summer of 1974. I am also grateful to my departmental colleagues for bearing with me through the alternating humors that are inevitable by-products of immersion in an artist as powerful as Berryman. Like anyone who studies this prolific poet I owe a special word of thanks to Richard J. Kelly and Ernest C. Stefanik, Jr., whose bibliographies have been constantly at my elbow. And I am grateful, in a way that those who admire his work will understand, to John Berryman, for teaching me things I did not know about love, about fear, and about myself.

Passages of this book appeared, in a different form, in *The Hollins Critic,* and are printed with the permission of Mr. John Rees Moore.

Quotations from the work are reprinted with the permission of Farrar, Straus & Giroux, Inc. from works by John Berryman: *Berryman's Sonnets,* Copyright © 1952, 1967 by John Berryman; *Delusions, Etc.,* Copyright © 1969, 1971 by John Berryman, Copyright © 1972 by the Estate of John Berryman; *The Dream Songs,* Copyright © 1959, 1962, 1963, 1964, 1965, 1966, 1967, 1968, 1969 by John Berryman; *Homage to Mistress Bradstreet,* Copyright © 1956 by John Berryman; *Love & Fame,* Copyright © 1970 by John Berryman; *Recovery,* Copyright © 1973 by the Estate of John Berryman; and *Short Poems,* Copyright © 1948, 1958, 1964 by John Berryman, copyright renewed 1976 by Kate Berryman. Permission to quote from *The Maze* by Eileen Simpson, copyright © 1975, is granted by Simon & Schuster, Inc. Quotations are reprinted by permission of Faber and Faber Ltd. from (a) *Selected Poems 1938–1968,* (b) *Homage to Mistress Bradstreet,* (c) *Love & Fame,* (d) *Berryman's Sonnets,* (e) *77 Dream Songs,* (f) *His Toy, His Dream, His Rest,* by John Berryman.

I am able to make from the springboard the great leap whereby I
pass into infinity, my back is like that of a tight-rope dancer, having been twisted in my childhood, hence I find this easy.

Kierkegaard, *Fear and Trembling*

Two such opposed Kings encamp them still,
In man as well as herbs, grace and rude will.

Shakespeare, *Romeo and Juliet*

I'm scared a only one thing, which is me,
from othering I don't take nothin, see,
for any hound dog's sake.

Henry House

Introduction

He could never be charged with the sort of foolish consistency
that is alleged to be the sign of a small mind. It is difficult, in fact,
to conceive of a life more filled with puzzling inconsistencies than
that of John Berryman. His incredible productivity, to suggest a
most obvious contradiction, seems to be completely at odds with
his thirty-year dependence on alcohol. An articulate man of enormous charm and personal magnetism, he was given to offending
individuals, and audiences, from one coast to the other. A be-
liever in monogamy, he married three times and, by his own admission, engaged in numerous adulterous liaisons. An inspired
teacher throughout his long career, he was, on some days, completely inaudible. A life-long Democrat, his candidate in 1968
was Nelson Rockefeller: "I plan to vote for him twice—once with
a black face and once with a white face. I may even go so far as to
shave off my beard, and then they'd let me vote for him a third
time, don't you think?" [1] And this unhappy man, who spent his
life lamenting the suicide that left him fatherless at age eleven,
jumped to his own death in 1972, leaving behind a young wife
and two daughters, aged eight and one.

The details of artists' lives have a strong attraction for us; this is especially true of a writer as brilliant, as troubled, and as flamboyant as Berryman. We are compelled to ask questions, some of which are probably unanswerable, about his erratic behavior and about the sources of his art. Did he, with the death of his father, suffer an irreversible loss, one that was to be the source of the guilt and despair that dominated his adult life? Can a man mourn a loss for nearly fifty years, or is such mourning merely an excuse for heavy drinking? Was it his loss of faith, following his father's suicide, that was in fact responsible for his lifelong anxiety? Was it his mother after all, as his posthumous novel suggests, who was the dominant person in his life? Was his preoccupation with fame a product of his insecurity? Were his classes and poetry readings, at times spellbinding and at times incoherent, an essential form of reinforcement? Did his sense of personal debasement also require reinforcement, thereby contributing to his behavior? Was he, as he suggests here and there in his work, latently homosexual? Are his *Dream Songs,* as Lewis Hyde insists, to be explained away as the self-pitying indulgences of a resentful alcoholic? [2] Would he have survived in a city with an intellectual climate different from that of Minneapolis? Is there anything anyone could have done to rescue him from himself? Was his suicide a deliberate act? Was it impulsive? Was it, like that of Hemingway, a response to physical and intellectual deterioration?

It is because Berryman produced work of major importance and because this work, more than that of most writers, merges with his life, that questions like these should be raised. Thus I do not want to shy away from biographical questions, even though this book is designed primarily as an introduction to the poetry. Until his unpublished papers—diaries, plays, essays, stories, journals—are made available, and his letters published, it will be difficult for anyone to provide a very persuasive picture of his inner life. We do have his unusually intimate poems, however, an extensive body of critical essays, and that odd autobiographical fragment called *Recovery*, and from these some tentative hypotheses can be drawn about the man, and about the relationship between his life and work. So, in the course of my readings I shall occasionally refer to details from the life, accepting responsibility for any sins of commission as well as for those of omission.

If his private world is still more or less inaccessible, there is nevertheless a good deal about Berryman that is a matter of public record. Let me begin an informal biographical sketch by describing four photographs, taken over a period of thirty-one years. The first, shot in 1940 at the time of his first major publication, shows a rather affected looking young man of 26 with furrowed brow, carefully combed short hair, and full brush mustache. His mouth is grim, the overall expression rather dour. In the second, taken twenty-two years later, the expression is nearly identical, with the eyes downcast, the mouth tight. Now, however, the 48-year-old writer, bespectacled and wearing a bow tie, his hair slightly mussed, looks like everyone's stereotypical professor, except that there is something vaguely disturbing, slightly haunted, about this scholarly face. In the third portrait, one of those taken in Ireland for *Life* by Terence Spencer in 1967, Berryman appears to have undergone a remarkable transformation. Here is a full-bearded man peering somewhat bemusedly through plastic spectacles; a brick ruin looming in the background makes him look like a pagan diety. The tight mouth has disappeared behind luxurious grey whiskers. The professor has clearly turned into a bard. In the final shot, taken in his last year, the beard is considerably less liberated, and the mouth, composed in what could be either a smile or a grimace, has reappeared. Smoke from a cigarette drifts past the right ear, and the light has caught his glasses so as to punctuate each eye with a bright dot. The head is tilted, the impression one of calm. This does not appear to be the face of a man looking into the abyss.

The subject in these photographs was born on October 25,

1914, in McAlester, a small Oklahoma town. Since he worked the scorpion into his poems it is not so frivolous to mention astrology as it might otherwise be. One is struck, conditioned cynicism about such matters notwithstanding, by the persuasive place in the poet's life of the conventional Scorpio characteristics: dominating personality; powerful, difficult individuality; secretiveness; ruthlessness; inconsistency; charisma. Born three days earlier he would have been an evenhanded Libra, and we would be without the more daring and passionate of his poems. Or so would say those who put their faith in celestial bodies. Picasso was also born on October 25.

Berryman's father was a banker named John Allyn Smith (the middle name often gets misprinted as Allen), his mother a school-teacher from St. Louis named Martha Little. (Smith and Little—an unprepossessing inheritance for a poet who was to put so much stock in nomenclature.) They met in an Oklahoma boarding house, and married because "they were the only people who could read and write for hundreds of miles around." [3] Martha Little Smith was something of a rebel, regarded as unfeminine by her decorous family in Missouri. Her singularly unrebellious desire, however, was to have a son, and she was finally "blessed with two, five years apart, with a daughter, who died, in between." [4] Late in his life Berryman said that the only thing he regretted more than having no gift for music was having no sister. [5]

For the first ten years of his life John Smith, Jr. lived in Anadarko and in other small Oklahoma villages—Lamar, Sasakwa, and Wagoner. Since the family never put down deep roots there was no childhood Eden to which the exiled poet could later dream of returning. His parents were Roman Catholic, and from the age of five he served at Mass and attended Catholic schools. When he was ten the family moved to Tampa, on the Florida west coast, and for the next year and a half John and his younger brother, Jefferson, did the things children do, such as collect stamps, swim, and listen to the sometimes violent quarrels of their parents. Their father was a difficult man who, concerned that his wife might leave him, sometimes threatened to swim out to sea with one of the boys, beyond the point where rescue was possible.[6] On June 26, 1926, he shot himself in the breast outside John's window. The boy, who was eleven, heard the shot. This, not surprisingly, was an event that would haunt him all his life, that would be the source of virtually unpurgeable despair and resentment. Smith was buried in Oklahoma. His widow took her sons to Gloucester, Massachusetts, and then to New York. There she married another banker, John Angus McAlpin Berryman, and young John, though he apparently feared and disliked the man, took his name, becoming John Allyn McAlpin Berryman. This marriage ended in divorce ten years later. The boy attended eighth grade at P.S. 69 in Jackson Heights, Long Island, and during this year wrote half a science-fiction book "about a trip to Neptune & Ee-loro-a'ala." [7] He then spent four unhappy years at South Kent School, a "muscular" high-church Episcopal prep school in the lovely northwest corner of Connecticut. There he gave up his Catholicism and, if we accept *Recovery* as autobiography, tried for the first time to take his own life: "Sucked off Dopey Compson in the tool-shed one winter afternoon, he made me do it. . . . Suicide-attempt lay down across the rails, train coming, hauled off." [8]

In the fall of 1932, then a very bright seventeen, and having completed his junior year, Berryman enrolled in Columbia College where, emerging from the prep school fog, he spent four memorable years. In his freshman year he ran the quarter and half mile, rowed on the freshman crew, joined the wrestling team, and lost an election (for class vice-president) as well as what was left of his religious faith. In his second year he joined the literary group (he later became editor of *Columbia Review*), wrote a

poem a day, some of which were published, and did some reviewing for *The Nation*. In 1934 he wrote a series of sonnets for
his mother's birthday. These have not yet been published. Mrs.
Berryman, now in her eighties, read them to me, and what I
heard is very cautious verse that nevertheless communicates a
good deal of strong feeling.[9] The young poet was beginning to
discover his powers.

During the New York years Berryman, like so many Columbia
men of his generation (including classmate Robert Giroux, who
was later to be his publisher), became a disciple of the kindly
Mark Van Doren, responding enthusiastically to *A Winter Diary*
(1935), and taking all of his courses; the powerful influence of Van
Doren had much to do with the fact that Berryman himself became a teacher-scholar-poet. In his junior year he contributed
eleven very conventional poems and three essays to the *Columbia Review*, and a poem and a review to *The Nation*. He failed
Van Doren's course in eighteenth-century literature because he
confessed, in an otherwise strong examination, to having read
only seventeen of the forty-two required books. After five months
of diligent work he passed the course and his scholarship was re-
stored. He also took a summer school course with Allen Tate,
who found him to be "somebody to talk *at*." [10] Their lives were
to intersect later, first in a joint attack on those who wanted to
deny Pound the Bollingen Prize, and later at the University of
Minnesota where Tate was one of the first Regents' Professors,
the title Berryman held at the time of his death.

In his senior year he published five poems and an essay on
Yeats in the *Review* (Giroux was editor), and wrote an essay on
R. C. Sherriff for *The Nation*. He was graduated Phi Beta Kappa
with a B.A. in 1936, the recipient of a Kellett Fellowship to study
at Clare College, Cambridge. (Before settling in England he took
a trip to Canada, grew his first beard, and summered in Heidel-
berg.) In looking back on his Cambridge years in 1970 he told

Richard Kostelanetz "I drew in my horns. I realized my stuff was no good." [11] Reading omnivorously, he was elected, after four three-hour examinations, a Charles Oldham Shakespeare Scholar, the first American to be so honored. He made a special pilgrimage to Ireland to take high tea with Yeats, and also met Auden as well as Dylan Thomas, who became a pub-crawling companion. "We used to play darts a lot at bars. I was much better than Thomas and I beat him all the time. Then he discovered that he was born one day before me. . . . He thought that was great. From then on, whenever I beat him at darts Thomas would look down at me and say 'a little more respect there, Berryman, a little more respect.' " [12] Thomas, who was in fact born two days after Berryman, was obviously amusing himself at the expense of his gullible American friend.

In his second year at Cambridge, Berryman reviewed books of poetry for *New York Herald Tribune Books,* and had poems accepted by important journals, including *The Southern Review* and *New Directions in Prose and Poetry.* During reading periods he travelled in France and Germany. After receiving a B.A. from Clare, he returned to New York and lived at his mother's home in Queens. (There is a story, possibly apocryphal, that he failed to get a job as an advertising copywriter partly because of his beard and partly because he innocently suggested that an insurance company adopt as its symbol the Rock of Gibraltar.) He met Delmore Schwartz, who was to become one of his closest friends, and served as poetry editor, for a year, of *The Nation.* In the fall of 1939 he moved to Detroit, where he spent a year as Instructor in English at Wayne State University, then called Wayne.

1940 was the year of his first important publication. Twenty of his poems, along with an earnest prose essay and the first of the photographs I have described, were published in *Five American Poets,* brought out by New Directions. Some of the work had previously appeared in prestigious journals, such as *The Kenyon*

Review and *Partisan Review*, but publication in a book was particularly heartening to the 26-year old poet, especially in that one of
the reviewers, Oscar Williams, announced that "the volume is at
its best in John Berryman . . . his imagery [is] controlled and
beautifully timed." [13] In this same year he wrote a provocative
review of Thomas' *The World I Breathe*, focusing on the literary
sources of his friend's work and ending with the surprising obser-
vation that the book "does not show the major signs, such as a
powerful dramatic sense, wide interests, a flexible and appropriate diction, skill over a broad range of subjects, that are clear in
the work of his American contemporary Delmore Schwartz and
point confidently to the future." [14] In the process of indicating
what he found lacking in Thomas, Berryman was clearly charting
the course he wanted his own work to take.

In the fall of the year he moved to Massachusetts to hold one of
the new Briggs-Copeland instructorships at Harvard. He remained for three years, teaching and continuing to publish poems
and criticism, e.g., "the worst poetry, then, and it is excruciating,
is by Charles Henri Ford, Paul Goodman, Eugene Golas, Hubert
Creekmore, and George Kauffman. Terrible also are the 'chain-
poems' written by the VOU club, the New Apocalypse Group,
and other misguided persons." [15] In 1942 New Directions
brought out 2,000 copies of *Poems* in its Poet of the Month
Series. Most of the work had appeared in journals, and one
poem, "The Statue," was reprinted from *Five Young American
Poets*. Northrop Frye dismissed the book as "constipated elegance," [16] but at least one American critic was impressed: "Berryman's collection is provocative, stirring up the right kind of
protest and slinging a straight arrow at social and political corruption." [17] The young poet had become an acknowledged member
of the American literary community.

On the day before his twenty-eighth birthday Berryman married Eileen Patricia Mulligan. The union lasted eleven years.

Some of the guilt that permeates the later work can probably be traced to his behavior during these years. His wife's view of the marriage is found in Eileen Simpson's *The Maze,* a roman à clef that provides a balanced and believable analysis of a manic, disreputable poet named Benjamin Bold. This is the most revealing study of the poet's personality in print. [18]

Twice rejected for service on medical grounds (his eyes and nerves were weak), Berryman continued teaching and writing throughout the war. In the fall of 1943, responding to an invitation from R. P. Blackmur, he settled in Princeton, where he remained intermittently until 1951. During this period he was a Fellow in Creative Writing, a Rockefeller Fellow (1944–46), a lecturer, and a Hodder Fellow. His students included the poet W. S. Merwin, the novelist Frederick Buechner, and the translator and critic William Arrowsmith.

In 1946 he wrote one of the perceptive, fully researched essays that is typical of his work as a critic. (The prose essays, many of which are superb, were published by Farrar, Straus & Giroux in 1976 with the title *The Freedom of the Poet.*) The occasion was a review of some recent books about Henry James, and it is clear that he read virtually all of James—he could not have taken F. O. Matthiessen to task for specific misreadings had he not done so. His general impression of the novelist is revealing: "Utterly as his world seems to have been clubbed down, he is the great novelist of our time whose experience speaks most directly to us; the experience of others is nearer, but they have not his authority or size." [19] One product of this immersion was a Jamesian story called "The Lovers," which first appeared in *The Kenyon Review* and was later republished in *Best American Short Stories,* 1946. Two other stories were published during Berryman's lifetime, "Thursday Out," in *The Noble Savage,* Spring 1961 (but written in 1958), and "The Imaginary Jew," which appeared in *The Kenyon Review* in Autumn 1945 (and was awarded first prize in the journal's story contest). In 1975 *American Review* published "Wash Far Away," a study of a professor working through a crisis. These stories, along with the previously unpublished "All Their Colours Exiled," are collected in *The Freedom of the Poet.* Another story, "Our Sins Are More Than We Can Bear," written during the Princeton years, appeared in the *Twin Cities Express,* October 1, 1973.

In 1946 Berryman also wrote an essay on Fitzgerald (for *Kenyon*) in which he quotes Chekhov's definition of grace: "When a man spends the least possible number of movements over some definite action, that is grace." This was actually a peculiarly graceless year for the 32-year old poet. He fell in love with a young married woman, and their affair was attended by the usual disruptions, deceptions, furtive meetings, euphoria, jealousy, and despair. It was during this year that the terrible problem with alcohol commenced. Berryman kept a journal of the relationship, a long poetic sequence that was to remain private until the publication, in 1967, of *Berryman's Sonnets.* He had always been the dominant half of his various relationships, but in sharp-tongued, hard drinking "Lise" he met an equal. When she refused to leave her husband to marry him he lapsed into a suicidal depression. At the urging of his wife (who did not know about the affair) he sought medical help, and remained in psychoanalysis from 1947 through 1953. According to William Martz, "the analysis relieved his suicidal depression and led him to renounce the affair; thereafter he still saw his analyst occasionally. At the time of his separation from his wife in 1953 . . . both were hoping for reconciliation." [20]

During the late '40s Berryman devoted any time he could spare from his poetry and teaching to a long and complex study of Stephen Crane. In 1948 he published his first major collection of poems, *The Dispossessed,* and was awarded the Guarantors and Levinson prizes, underwritten by *Poetry* magazine. In April 1949

"The Poetry of Ezra Pound" was published in *Partisan Review*. The essay was written as the introduction to *Ezra Pound: Selected Poems* (New Directions), but, according to J. M. Linebarger, was rejected by Pound and by James Laughlin as not suitable for "young readers." [21] When the Library of Congress, this same year, decided to discontinue the Bollingen Prize following the uproar attending its presentation to *Pisan Cantos*, Berryman and Tate circulated a letter that was published in *The Nation* with the signatures of seventy-three writers, mostly poets. The battle was won by the pro-Pound forces when the Bollingen Foundation decided to continue the prize, with the same judges, under the aegis of Yale University. Berryman himself received the award in 1969.

Stephen Crane was published in 1950 by William Sloane Associates as part of the American Men of Letters Series. The book, which continues to elicit admiration and hostility from Crane scholars, is not a conventional biography, nor is it a reading of the work in the usual sense. It is, rather, a psychoanalytical study, the analyses of the prose and poetry invariably deriving their conclusions from Berryman's sense of the writer's inner life. The central thesis is indicated in a quotation from John Butler Yeats: "Art comes only when there is *abandon* and a world of dreaming and waiting and passionate meditation." [22] The study is useful not only for its insights on Crane but also for what it reveals about Berryman: "We have met Henry Fleming and Henry Johnson, and we shall meet a Henry stranger still, later on."

The year this book was published Berryman was a lecturer at the University of Washington in Seattle, was the recipient of a grant from the National Institute of Arts and Letters, and won an award from the American Academy. During the next academic year, 1951–52, he was Elliston lecturer in poetry at the University of Cincinnati, and wrote, for *The Hudson Review*, one of his most important critical studies, "Shakespeare at 30." (At the time of his death he had been awarded a Guggenheim Fellowship to continue his work on a book to be called "Shakespeare's Reality.") He also published a splendid introduction to Matthew Lewis' *The Monk* (in an edition brought out by Grove Press), in the course of which he gives a sharp picture of himself as "the American writer confronting many nervous persons at the end of the day's abstract work collected in a fireless, carefully empty room, smoking cigarettes and drinking martinis; envying, perhaps, abductions, duels, not to mention spectres and the Old One's agents." Another of the peculiar pleasures of this essay is the demonstration of his zeal for discovering, among much poor stuff, lines of poetry that struck his fancy:

> Time flies, and still they weep, for never
>   The fugitive can time restore:
> An hour once fled, has fled for ever,
>   And all the rest shall smile no more! [23]

Berryman was awarded his first Guggenheim Fellowship, for 1952–53, to work on his long poetic tribute to Anne Bradstreet. Part of the year was spent in Rome, where he met William and Rose Styron and saw much of Theodore Roethke. The two also met in London, and during one session of pub-crawling Berryman got lost and "wandered the streets all night long." [24] Toward the end of 1953 "Homage to Mistress Bradstreet" was published, without notes, in *Partisan Review*. In the following year the poet gave a course during the summer session at Harvard. One of his students was the gifted essayist and novelist Edward Hoagland, who describes the experience: "He taught by exemplitude. He talked mostly about books he had loved with a fever that amounted to a kind of courage. He hated stupidity and was harsher to lazy students than any teacher I've ever known, but he was also affectionate toward promising writers. He cared so much for literature." [25] It was his eloquence and passion that accounted for his reputation as a superb teacher. Inconsistent and unpredictable, as are most high-powered classroom performers, he was capable of following a dazzling presentation with a class singularly stale and flat. Toward the end of his career he sometimes failed to lecture at all, reading, instead, often inaudibly, from the books assigned.[26] During his good years, however, at his best, he was by all reports a persuasive, thoroughly prepared, and exciting teacher, adored by large numbers of devoted students. His beautiful story "Wash Far Away" reveals how seriously he took his role as teacher, and suggests how much he cared about his students.

The central place in his life as a scholar-teacher was the University of Minnesota. He and Eileen moved to Minneapolis in 1955. Before doing so, however, he taught briefly at the University of Iowa. This was, according to William Dickey, a chaotic time for the poet, one that ended in confusion, bitterness, and a sudden departure. As Mr. Dickey puts it:

> I was astonished when, a few years later, as a junior instructor at Cornell I was asked to lunch to meet Mark Van Doren . . . and found that something very strange had happened to history. Van Doren recounted with interest what Berryman had told him: how, having accepted a position at the University of Iowa, he had boarded the train from Chicago, reached Iowa City, looked out at the dismal railway station and the little town behind it, and had gone straight on to Minneapolis without ever getting off the train. Berryman had edited his life, he had removed some six months from it as one might remove a feverish appendix, and it seemed to me that in doing so he had removed or edited some of my life too.[27]

Mr. Dickey recalls the experience of having a poem "held out at the length of an indignant arm over a seminar table, and hearing a voice filled with a sort of wrathful incredulity saying: 'Now what are we to make of this ridiculous poem?' "[28]

At Minnesota Berryman began as a lecturer in the Department

of Humanities (separate from the Department of English) and at the time of his death, seventeen years later, was a Regents' Professor. He gave courses on "The European Heritage" (the Renaissance and the Reformation, for example), on the history of ideas, on Christian origins and the Middle Ages, on American civilization, on New Testament criticism, and on Shakespeare, Dante, and other writers. "If poets teach," he said, "they ought not teach poetry. That's too much like the main thing, poetry and criticism; it can be comforting and yet cheapening. A writer never does the same thing twice; but a teacher is bound to his routine." [29] He regarded his work as a scholar (and his critical essays and scholarly editions are extremely impressive in quantity and quality) to be of equal importance with his career as an imaginative writer.

Minneapolis itself is an all-American city, and hence one in which Berryman, though it gradually became home, often felt himself to be something of an outsider, an Eastern visitor. In a poem called "MPLS, MOTHER" (*Minneapolis Tribune*, December 1, 1974), written in 1970 and not included in *Delusions, Etc.*, he expresses some good-natured reservations about the "essential nonentity" of this "site without history," this "place of great winds": "Vast eyesore granaries, pathetic monopoly newspapers . . . Even on *this* continent, I prefer Mexico D. F., / & Cinti Ohio, so near above Kentucky; / & suddenly since World War II unrecognizable & unbearable New York." Some aspects of Minneapolis life were clearly alien to his New York-educated soul. Low on pollution and high on outdoor activities, the city is surrounded by lovely parks and lakes (though "only the Lake of the Isles," he writes, "possesses distinction"), and in the summer wholesome-looking, bronzed Minneapolitans of all ages can be seen jogging, rowing, bicycling, swimming, and generally not sitting still. In the winter these inhabitants tend to settle into their comfortable homes; like all very cold places, the city has a reputation for heavy drinking. There is a good deal of cultural activity, certainly enough for any but the most gluttonous appetite. There are those (mostly easterners) who claim that the place is bland, but its citizens are more than willing to sacrifice a bit of urban exoticism and ethnic variety for the good midwestern life.

Berryman's Minneapolis actually was somewhat exotic, having as its centers of gravity a distinguished university with its heterogeneous faculty, and a galaxy of atmospheric bars (The Brass Rail, The Masters, The Bedford) with their peculiar ambiance and mixed populations. In his non-tavern world he was blessed with a number of close friends—people of wit, learning, accomplishment, and understanding. And with the purchase of a modest but comfortable wooden house on Arthur Avenue (after having spent most of his adult life in unprepossessing rented apartments) he finally became a Minneapolitan proper. The pleasant metropolis and its great university provided, in all, a measure of welcome and support that Berryman probably would not have found anywhere else in the country.

In his second year in the city, 1956, three events importantly affected his life: Farrar, Straus & Giroux brought out *Homage to Mistress Bradstreet,* he was divorced from Eileen and, now 42, he married a young woman named Ann Levine. A son, Paul, was born in 1957, and later in the year the family spent two months in India, where Berryman served as U.S. Specialist for the State Department on loan to U.S.I.S., lecturing and giving readings. The fruits of this trip are a handful of dream songs and the prose narrative describing a visit to the Taj Mahal, "Thursday Out," published in Saul Bellow's short-lived journal, *The Noble Savage.*

In 1958 C. Fredericks, a small publishing firm in Pawlet, Vermont, published a handsome white pamphlet (dedicated to Ann Levine), called *His Thought Made Pockets & The Plane Buckt,* the title comically suggesting Berryman's willingness to assume the burden of guilt for virtually everything. The collection, which consists of thirteen poems, was limited to 526 copies. Some of the work had appeared in *Partisan Review, Poetry, American Letters, The New Yorker,* and the *Virginia Quarterly Review.* Also included are "some pieces of an old poem called 'The Black Book,' " a work in progress that was to remain fragmentary.

In 1960, then 46, Berryman was divorced again. He spent part of the year as Visiting Professor at Berkeley, and saw two books through the press—one, *The Art of Reading,* with his Minnesota colleagues Ralph Ross and Allen Tate (Berryman contributed essays on Babel, Hemingway, Crane, and Eliot), the other a paperback edition of Thomas Nashe's *The Unfortunate Traveler,* in the introduction to which he attacks Eliot's "intolerable and perverse theory of the impersonality of the artist." The following year he married for the third time. His wife, an attractive Minneapolitan named Kathleen Donohue, was 22. She changed her name, at his request, to Kate. Two daughters were born to the couple, Martha ("Twissy") in 1963, and Sarah Rebecca in 1971. During the first year of this marriage Berryman was Visiting Lecturer at the School of Letters, Indiana University. The following year he was writer-in-residence at Brown University, filling in for Edwin Honig, who was on leave. He taught at Bread Loaf, in Vermont, during the summer and, in spite of missing classes, was cherished by his students, who took particular delight in his impromptu poetry recitals at parties. In the fall of 1963 he returned to Minneapolis.

For some years, "dream songs" had been appearing in various journals. *The Noble Savage* for February 1960, for example, published a group of twelve, including the entertaining "The jolly old man is a silly old dumb," later dropped from the collection. There were "Nine Dream Songs" in *Poetry* for October–November 1963, along with a note that "all will appear in his book 75 Dream Songs soon to be published. . . ." Others appeared in *The Times Literary Supplement, The New York Review of Books, The Kenyon Review,* and elsewhere. *77 Dream Songs* was published in 1964, with a dedication to his wife and to Saul Bellow, and with the note that the book constitutes sections "of a poem in progress." It was reviewed, often intelligently, by such influential critics as Louis Martz, Adrienne Rich, John Malcolm Brinnin, M. L. Rosenthal, Christopher Ricks, and Philip Toynbee. "This great Pierrot's universe," Robert Lowell wrote, "is more tearful and funny than we can easily bear." [30] The work was awarded the Pulitzer Prize for Poetry in 1965.

In 1966 Berryman and his family flew to Dublin, where he spent the year (as a Guggenheim Fellow) writing more songs and pub-crawling. He returned to New York for ten days to receive the prestigious $5,000 Academy of American Poets Fellowship. In 1967 his publisher brought out *Short Poems*, which draws together *The Dispossessed, His Thought Made Pockets,* and a ponderous "Formal Elegy" on the death of John Kennedy. *Berryman's Sonnets* also appeared that year. And he received a $10,000 award from the National Endowment for the Arts.

The following year also saw the publication of two books, *Homage to Mistress Bradstreet And Other Poems* in a Noonday Paperback, important because it represents a winnowing of the short poems, and *His Toy, His Dream, His Rest,* consisting of 308 songs that complete the major work. Again the songs received a good deal of attention, including a front page essay by Helen Vendler in *The New York Times Book Review,* and reviews by Karl Shapiro, Christopher Ricks, and others. The work won the National Book Award in 1969, the same year Berryman was selected to share the Bollingen Book Award with Karl Shapiro. Farrar, Straus & Giroux immediately brought the songs out in a single volume.

In 1970 Berryman published *Love & Fame,* a collection of often shocking autobiographical poems in which he dispenses with his persona, Henry, and speaks directly as, and about, himself. The book took a drubbing from some critics, a fact in no way lost on a poet who was thin-skinned about what he regarded as insensitive reviews (he responded, in print, to Hayden Carruth's review in *The Nation*), and who had a lifelong preoccupation with public approbation and its accouterments. In the fall of 1970, just before the book appeared, he gave a reading at the State University of New York at Brockport. His host, William Heyen, has written an absorbing memoir of the hectic two days, one that gives a vivid picture of an extraordinarily vulnerable poet toward the end of his life. Heyen comments on the chain smoking, constant bourbon (water, no ice), insomnia, crying jags, desire to talk for hours, and on the preoccupation with dead friends. He realized that Berryman was constantly driving himself toward a new poem "in a necessary frenzy," noting that he perpetually jotted down phrases, recited lines, and pulled one or another of his new poems out of a pocket, frequently protesting, "Isn't that good? Isn't that good?" Describing his guest as "charming, disputatious, dominating, brilliant," Heyen reveals his feelings following Berryman's departure after forty-eight nonstop hours: "As his plane took off, I cried. Exhaustion and relief. I'd never been through anything like that before. I know that I felt, after he left Brockport, that he would not live for long. . . ." [31]

During the next year Berryman (who had a grant from the National Endowment for the Humanities to work on a biography of Shakespeare) was in and out of St. Mary's Hospital, an imposing structure that looms over the Mississippi River. (According to his good friend Dr. Boyd Thomes he always referred to the place as "Werewolf Hills.") He remained for several weeks at a time as part of a therapy group that used as its strategy for cure the twelve steps formulated by Alcoholics Anonymous, a procedure requiring one to believe that only "a Power greater than ourselves could restore us to sanity." (Step Three: "Made a decision to turn our will and our lives over to the care of God as we understood Him.") The treatment involves, among other things, a great deal of public confession. During these stays he began to write, on contract, the thinly veiled autobiographical novel that was published, unfinished, after his death. He also completed, and read proof for, his final book of poems.

On January 7, 1972, aged 57, Berryman flung himself about 100 feet toward the west bank of the Mississippi River, jumping from the railing of the bridge that joins the two parts of the university campus. Before doing so he removed his glasses and, according to a witness, gave a tentative wave of his hand. He had no identification on him save for a blank check. The body was recovered from the frozen rocks on which it landed. There was no explicit foreshadowing of the act—as Robert Giroux has said, just seven months earlier not only was his friend preparing his essays for publication and getting a new child christened, but "he was planning a half-dozen further books to be written through the 1970s." [32] These books included his "third epic," to be called *The Children.* Berryman's conduct during the days just preceding the suicide was not, according to his friends, exceptional, though his usual behavior, characterized by a constant state of nearly unbearable nervous agitation, would be exceptional in most persons. Throughout his life he was, by all reports, a dynamo of unpurgeable energy (Van Doren says that as a student Berryman was "high-strung, nervous, intense . . . and sometimes seemed to be composed of nothing but bristles and points"),[33] and the easiest explanation of the suicide is that he simply could no longer endure to inhabit his body, that the tension, physical and emotional, was too intense to bear.

Easy explanations, though, satisfy no one; we are left only with questions and, until his biography appears, with little expectation of answers. (An authorized life, to be published by Farrar, Straus & Giroux, is being prepared by John Haffenden.) From a summary of any individual's life, however, certain details will emerge as crucial. In this case it is clear that his emotional responses were shaped by his close relationship with both of his parents, by his parents' relationship with each other, and by his father's death. It is also likely that as a lapsed Catholic he suffered a deep sense of unworthiness and loss (even in his later years he continued, sporadically, to attend Mass). His discovery of a surrogate father in Mark Van Doren, following a relatively numbing adolescence, gave him the sort of initiation into the mysteries of literature without which he might well have become a stockbroker or banker. His marriages to young women appear to be attempts to impose some order on the chaos of his life, to domesticate a wild and ruffian spirit. And his addiction to alcohol, certainly a major fact of his final tense decades, was a source of his art and a cause of his personal hell. At once stabilizer and destroyer, midwife and coroner, focuser and depressant, it became the daily equivalent of Shakespeare's lust, "Had, having, and in quest to have extreme; / A bliss in proof; and proved, a very woe; / Before, a joy proposed; behind, a dream."

Alcohol is the source and the subject of much of Berryman's most provocative work, and given his emotional vulnerability there was little likelihood of his overcoming the addiction. Lewis Hyde blames all of us for this failure: "We did not handle him well. Few of his critics faced the death in these poems . . . in the future it would be nice if it were a little harder for the poet to come to town drunk and have everyone think it's great fun." [34] Perhaps. It seems unlikely, though, that anyone who encountered Berryman during his times of greatest illness thought it was much fun. He had a habit of calling his friends (and critics) in the early hours of the morning to share a just-completed poem, and was invariably surprised and hurt when his mood was not shared. During his reading tours, moreover, he frequently left his hosts (such as William Heyen) as well as his audiences (when he actually got to the auditorium) in a state of emotional distress. Finally, despite his unbelievable constitution, he himself could bear no more. No man knows another's temptations very well; we do not yet know enough about the death of this gifted man to assign blame. We know for certain only that his temptations were many, that they were compelling, and that one of them, the desire for self-destruction, was on a particularly cold day in 1972 satisfied.

CHAPTER 1

The Short Poems

An entertainer, a Molière, in the onset
under too nearly Mozart's aegis,
the mysteries of Oedipus old were not beyond you.
                    "Beethoven Triumphant"

I

That Berryman is frequently linked with Robert Lowell as one of
the two most significant poets of his generation can be accounted
for almost wholly on the basis of his two major sequences. When
Edmund Wilson described *Homage to Mistress Bradstreet* as the
most important long poem since *The Waste Land*, its creator had
clearly surfaced from the group of gifted but relatively minor
writers who were his contemporaries. The dramatic reception
given *The Dream Songs* enhanced this position, and though Berryman had been publishing for over twenty years he quickly became identified—through its prominence in the classroom, in
anthologies, and in literary histories—almost exclusively with the
Songs. Despite the publication in 1967 of *Short Poems,* most of

the earlier poetry, both the apprentice work and that with artistic merit, has been relegated to a kind of limbo by the prominence of the sequences.

After a sustained period of research and reading a critic often comes to regard as significant even the most unexceptional work of a writer in whom he has developed a professional interest. This may be, of course, because he needs to justify an expenditure of spirit by insisting that its object is worthy of the effort. In other cases, however, an undiscriminating response is not so much an attempt to elevate the artist as it is an expression of the critic's own sensibility—we are, after all, attracted to those writers who speak to us. In my own case, what first drew me to Berryman was his experimentation with the long sequence, and I admit outright that most of the work of the 1940s (and late 1930s) appeals to me primarily because of its relationship to the later books. I cannot, therefore, provide a revisionist essay, will not insist that the quintessential Berryman is waiting to be discovered in the heretofore undervalued early poems. I do want to comment on these poems, however, and in some detail, partly because they do indeed prepare the way for the later books and partly because some of the work actually has endured on its own.

Who is Mary Bernard? Who is George Marion O'Donnell? Had Berryman stopped writing in 1940 he would be as little known as these poets, both of whom appear with him in *Five Young American Poets,* published by New Directions in 1940. There is nothing in the book, including the frequently anthologized "Winter Landscape," to suggest the remarkable flowering to follow. Nor is there anything by one of the other poets represented to suggest that he would develop in important ways. In the review of the book in which he praises Berryman, Oscar Williams dismisses this other poet as "the re-write man, the intellectual hotcha, the will-to-be-a-poet with no talent." [1] He is talking about Randall Jarrell. The fifth contributor, W. R. Moses, published his first book of poems (*Identities*) in 1965, and a second (*Passage*) in 1976, both with Wesleyan University Press.

The five poets are all products of their time, and a grim time it was, for new poetry and for a good many other things. The Berryman selections—ominous, flat, social, indistinctly allusive, exhausted, preceded by a stiff essay on the nature of poetry—give a good indication of how representative his art was at the time. They also provide a look at some early attempts to deal with the themes that would preoccupy him throughout his career. The twenty poems, written during his early twenties, mostly in England, give clear evidence of his literary debts (the collection is an echo chamber) as well as of his slavish adherence to conventional forms. A typical Berryman poem of the period organizes itself into stanzas, often of eight or nine lines, with a carefully worked out rhyme scheme. There is a pervasive, generally stultifying reliance on iambic pentameter; some of the work seems to have been composed by a well-programmed computer with Weltschmerz. The speaker, typically, is seated in a room at dusk, alone in thought, brooding about the dangerous reality beyond his walls, all the while making disturbing connections between this public world, with its nightmarish history and uncertain future, and his own private world, haunted by fears and spectres. Certain images appear over and over, invariably related to disease, darkness, fear, exhaustion, inaction, sleeplessness.

Let me be more specific about the work's characteristics. "Meditation," written in Cambridge when Berryman was 23 (and published originally in *The Southern Review*) is stiff, important, full of high sentence:

> The clenched lip, a wrinkle on the forehead
> Of hanging Christ; the eye sees everywhere
> Indestructible evidence of dread,
> In apples and in smiles, horrible both.

> But generosity upon her mouth
> Levels all torment in an actual tear.

In "The Trial," a hopeless Job expresses significant intellectual despair, again through fairly stiff iambs, this time in modified terza rima. The poem is dry and bitter, sicklied over with a pale cast of thought. Since its anguish is not grounded in any specific reality, the reader, while willing perhaps to accept its validity for the writer or speaker, is finally unable to participate in its feeling. "Letter to His Brother," the earliest of the works to survive the winnowing that preceded *Short Poems*, while typically elegiac and world-weary, is less abstract, more personal, and therefore considerably more accessible. It employs slant rhyme (waking ears—travellers; left—laughed), which was to become a Berryman trademark, and also introduces, for the first time in his published work, the sins-of-the-father motif:

> From the violent world our fathers brought,
> For which we pay with fantasy at dawn,
> Dismay at noon, fatigue, horror by night.

Relating the public world (Dachau) to the private, it is both eloquent and disturbing. "World-Telegram," an Audenesque summary of a day's grotesque news, includes the chilling image of a boy, "small, frightened, in a Sea Scout uniform," watching as his father is crushed by a ten-ton truck. The spectre of John Smith hovers at the margin of many of these early poems.

"Winter Landscape," the best known of the works in this selection, provides good examples of both the virtues and shortcomings of Berryman's early voice. A commentary on Peter Brueghel's "Hunters in the Snow," it is tightly organized into five-line stanzas, all in regular iambic pentameter, with two seemingly random rhymes. It is actually in blank verse, with stanza breaks serving to reinforce the impression of parts making up a whole, appropriate in a poem modelled on a painting. Since the poem is composed in one flowing sentence (a colon near the middle separates the details of presentation from the philosophical speculations that emerge), one reads the lines as one might look at the painting, the eye moving rapidly from detail to detail and not coming to a complete rest until the composition has been seen in its entirety.

Although its general intentions are admirable (Berryman was responding to Yeats' seductive rhetoric and to the hysterical political atmosphere of the period) the work is flawed by a ponderous, sententious tone. In his version of the painting, in *Pictures from Brueghel*, William Carlos Williams presents concrete details and lets the reader infer any cosmic implications. Where Williams renders, however, Berryman states, giving oracular significance to the discovery that life is short, art long. The high seriousness and the solemn trumpeting of the obvious are most damaging in the central stanza, with its inflated references to "the sandy time to come" and to "the evil waste of history / Outstretched." In the future, the poet says, the men in the painting, immutable as figures on an urn, will say "What place, what time, what morning occasion / Sent them into the wood." This all sounds so incontrovertibly profound that one is reluctant not to share the poet's mood. Berryman has failed, however, to provide compelling reasons for us to do so. The pictorial details are vivid and resonant, but they do not support the philosophical burden laid on them. The tone of insistent significance is particularly damaging in the line, "These men, this particular three in brown." The poet protests too much and too often.

This problem, of failing to discover an objective correlative, thus requiring that a particular image carry too heavy a metaphysical weight, is apparent in another much-anthologized poem about art and history, "The Statue," equally afflicted with bromidic moralizing. Composed of seven eight-line stanzas, with tetrameter fourth lines the only variation on the pentameter pattern, it is tightly made, each stanza completing a thought. The statue, like the Brueghel hunters, is the poem's symbolic center, the locus of details that radiate outward. Its dead eyes, like those of Fitzgerald's Dr. Eccleberg, look cynically across a cityscape of failure, frustration, and defeat. Again, time ravages the flesh but not the artifact. And man is oblivious to his fate: "The lovers pass. Not one of them can know / Or care which Humboldt is immortalized." As in the Brueghel poem the mood of wise resignation and world-weariness is difficult to share, at least for a contemporary sensibility that wants bromides presented, if at all, with some wit, some ambiguity, or at least with some ironic distance. The clay feet of "The Statue" are most apparent in the final stanza, in which the archness and obviousness, until then held at least somewhat in check, give way to an expression of adolescent sentimentality that transforms the poem into an embarrassing cliché:

> Beyond, the dark apartment where one summer
> Night an insignificant dreamer,
> Defeated occupant, will close his eyes
> Mercifully on the expensive drama
> Wherein he wasted so much skill, such faith,
> And salvaged less than the intolerable statue.

Ten of the twenty poems published in the New Directions Anthology were reprinted, eight years later, in *The Dispossessed.* They are also found in *Short Poems,* and thus comprise a permanent part of the Berryman canon. The excised poems are, for the most part, the more allusive and derivative of the group, with Yeats, Ransom, Auden, Hart Crane, and Van Doren the most obvious sources. (Yeats saved Berryman from the overwhelming influences of Eliot and Pound.) The poet also chose to relegate to oblivion two overtly topical poems ("Nineteen Thirty-Eight" and "The Apparition") that now seem more dated than anything

Auden removed from his own canon. None of the deleted work is so successful as the best of the poems retained, such as "World-Telegram," "Conversation," and "Parting as Descent." That Berryman chose to salvage "The Statue" and "Winter Landscape" is perhaps understandable. That anthologists have persisted in giving their blessing to these works suggests nothing so much as a high tolerance for inflated language.

II

Berryman's debut in *Five Young American Poets* was followed two years later by a solo volume, *Poems*, published in 2,000 copies by New Directions in its "Poet of the Month" series. The eleven lyrics in this pamphlet were written during 1939 and 1940, and most had already appeared in periodicals. "The Statue" is the only work chosen from the earlier New Directions collection. The pamphlet as a whole, which is very curious, serves to illustrate both the ways in which Berryman's poetry at this stage of his career is utterly unexceptional and the kinds of inhibitions he had to break through to discover an original style. *Poems* has practically no voice at all; it could have been written by any one of a score of post-Yeats-Eliot-Auden writers confronting the political realities of 1939. The reason for this absence of a unique presence, of a special language, is that the poet, dealing with ideas and politics, almost wholly ignores his feelings. I say almost, and the qualification is important. The volume is dedicated to Bhain Campbell, a friend (and Detroit roommate) who died of cancer in 1940 at the age of 29, and who is mentioned in *The Dream Songs* and in *Love & Fame*. The eloquent dedication verse is deeply felt, as are the two poems, "A Poem for Bhain" and "Epilogue," that end the pamphlet. "Epilogue" closes with the line "Nouns, verbs do not exist for what I feel," and this admission helps account for the odd absence of poems that express emotion. The closest Berryman comes to producing the obligatory conventional love lyric of a young poet, in fact, is in these elegies and in the section of "At Chinese Checkers" about his friend Delmore Schwartz. The poems that are framed by the Campbell tributes, stoical, derivative, and technically competent, are almost entirely lacking in emotional power.

Certain characteristics that dominate the work help account for its sterility. One is the introduction of topical events that assumes a conditioned response from the politically sympathetic reader—1 September 1939, Detroit, the Belgian surrender. Another, borrowed from Yeats ("Did she put on his knowledge with his power / Before the indifferent beak could let her drop?") is the significant unanswered question that has as its principal function the resurrection of sagging lines:

> *Who gave the order on the wall?*
> "River Rouge, 1932"

> What pride was active in that gorgeous sky?
> What dreadful leniency compelled the men
> Southward, the crumpled men?
>   "At Chinese Checkers"

> Whose is the version that will not appall?
>   "A Point of Age"

Another verbal mannerism, learned from Auden, is the capitalized abstraction: "Our Man of Fear," "the God Exaggeration," "The Hero." There are phrases throughout the book which, if not quite clichés, are flat, tired, ordinary: "Our dear upholstered memories," "the midnight of the mind," "the chromium luxury of the age." And there are passages that seem to be filched from other poets, from Yeats, for example:

> Venus on the half-shell was found a dish
> To madden a fanatic: from the nave
> Rolled obloquy and lust. Sea without fish . . .
> > "At Chinese Checkers"

Or from Auden on Yeats, by way of Eliot:

> . . . It was a cold night,
> People put on their wraps, the troops were cold
> No doubt, despite the calendar, no doubt
> Numbers of refugees coughed, and the sight
> Or sound of some killed others. A cold night.
> > "The Moon and the Night and the Men"

The political version of the fine old ballad "Lord Randall" ("O tell
me of the Russians, Communist, my son! / Tell me of the Russians, my honest young man!") is an example of the sort of one-
shot cleverness one finds in undergraduate literary journals.

The book, in short, is not very impressive. The major poem, a
119-line sequence about turning 25, called "A Point of Age," contains several powerful stanzas, and these redeem the collection
somewhat. Even in this poem, however, one gets the impression
of a sensibility that is blocked off from a sense of its personal
needs, that speaks instead for a generation. For all his references
to heartbreak, fear, sorrow, and hate the poem's speaker appears
to be far more aware of civic woe than of his own. It is hard to
believe that this voice would modulate into that of Henry Pussycat, a creature for whom nothing in the world is more important, newsworthy, or in an odd way, universal than his own private sorrows. Poetry of feeling, of course, is not necessarily more
powerful than poetry of social awareness, but it is clearly more
compatible with Berryman's gifts. It took him a great many years
to realize this. He was in his early work as thoroughly the prod-

uct of the Age of Anxiety as he was later on the product, and victim, of the Age of Catharsis.

III

The process of liberating his voice, a process that accelerated in *Mistress Bradstreet* and then culminated in *The Dream Songs,* was actually begun by Berryman in two books that preceded his dialogue with Anne Bradstreet, *The Dispossessed,* published in 1948, and the poetic journal written during 1946 and published as *Berryman's Sonnets* in 1967. "Dispossession" works on two levels for him, the first having to do with being deprived of one's place or possessions, the second indicating that one has been "relieved, saved, un-deviled, de-spelled." [2] This second activity, a form of exorcism, need not necessarily be a consummation devoutly to be wished, since the devil cast out may be life itself. (The fate of young Miles at the completion of *The Turn of the Screw* is a case in point, i.e., "his little heart, dispossessed, had stopped.") In any case, the title poem does not appear until the end of the book, and there it suggests both a sense of loss and a resolution, albeit tentative, to the sorts of questions raised in an earlier poem called "The Possessed," and in others as well. This is, for the most part, a spectre-haunted work by a poet who is seeking salvation from his memories, from the animal within, from various ghosts, and from an unendurable Weltanschauung.

The sense of hopelessness about the state of the world comes through unambiguously in poem after poem. Adams was right about history approaching a speechless end, the poet says. Certain phrases, chosen nearly at random from several poems, suggest the intensity and dimension of his political despair: "Disfigurement is general"; "none of us is well"; "the violent world";

"the world's decay"; "bitter and exhausted ground"; "a dying race." These are the nocturnal conclusions of a man who sees society being destroyed by a sick generation. And if the world out there is violent and ill, so is the one within—as one of his speakers puts it, "We breed up in our own breast our worse wars." Faced with the holocaust the poet composes lines that are troubled, humorless, consistently bleak.

Images of night run persistently through this gloomy book, and relate to the brooding sensibility at its center. He associates sunlight and daytime with art, the spirit, and the intellect. Night and darkness are related to the disturbances of man, be they political or sensual (though at this point in Berryman's work the senses are still in harness). And there are so many occasions of night falling or of a night wind rising that these devices finally function as a sort of *deus ex nocturna*, a way of giving resonance and mystery to lines that otherwise might remain coldly intellectual:

> The fog is settling and the night falls, sad. . .
>> "A Point of Age"

> The equine hour rears, no further friend. . .
>> "The Possessed"

> The night is on these hills, and some can sleep.
>> "Letter to his Brother"

> The car devoured the darkness, the moon hung,
> Blood over the pines, and the cold wind sang. . .
>> "Travelling South"

> The altering winds are dark and the winds blow. . .
>> "At Chinese Checkers"

> The inexhaustible prospect of the night. . .
>> "The Animal Trainer" (1)

> The moon came up late and the night was cold
>> "The Moon and the Night and the Men"

In addition to sharing repeated, ritualistic, lighting and sound effects, the lines are also indistinguishable rhythmically; any one stanza could be substituted for any other without causing the slightest structural disruption. This is revealing, since it points up just how conventional Berryman's rhythms are at this point, and since rhythm, more than anything else, is what distinguishes one poet from another, just how conventional a poet he was. In the first three sections of the book (all composed before 1943) there are only a few lines that do not have an unsubtle, singularly uninteresting iambic beat. A very high percentage of the lines, moreover, compose themselves with monotonous regularity into pentameters. Nevertheless, the book is technically interesting and even shows flashes of originality. This is because of Berryman's versatility in the use of stanzaic patterns and because of his extraordinarily skillful use of complex rhyme schemes, many of which employ approximate rhymes to good effect. The collection contains rhyming couplets, terza rima, blank verse, regularly rhymed four-line stanzas (for the most part comprising the weakest work), and variously rhymed stanzas of from six to nine lines. There are also two poems that have no regular stanzaic pattern, and two that effectively employ a diminishing pattern, each successive stanza losing a line.

Berryman at this stage was most comfortable, particularly in the longer sequences such as "Boston Common" and "At Chinese Checkers," with the Yeatsian eight-line stanza. Fourteen of the book's poems fall into the pattern, though no two use the same rhyme scheme. This stanza, like the octave of a sonnet, affords both rigorous formal constraints and room for considerable flexibility, permitting the technically facile craftsman to create the illusion of freedom within a rigorously circumscribed space. Given his attraction to and success with the stanza it is understandable that he chose it for *Homage to Mistress Bradstreet*. The work of *The Dispossessed*, moreover, looks ahead even further in time: the nine "Nervous Songs" (inevitably, for one especially responsive to the later Berryman, the most successful section of the book) introduce for the first time the extended sonnet that was to become the vehicle of the *Songs,* the eighteen-line lyric composed of three self-contained but fluid six-line stanzas.

The list of dark-and-wind lines may give the impression that the language of the book is of a piece. These lines are actually all from the first four sections, and I should round out the picture by quoting as well two brief passages from the fifth section, the seven poems of which were written in 1947 and 1948:

> Rising wind rucks from the sill
> The slack brocade beside   the old throne he dreams on.
> > "The Long Home"

> Glade grove & ghyll of antique childhood glide
> Off; from our grown grief, weathers that appal . . .

> Foul sleet ices the twigs, the vision frays . . .
> > "A Winter-Piece to a Friend Away"

The metamorphosis is remarkable, completely reversing that of Robert Lowell, who progressed from the baroque diction of *The Mills of the Kavanaughs* to a more idiomatic and natural speech (that favored by Williams) in his later books, starting with *Life Studies.* Reading straight through *The Dispossessed* one moves suddenly from language that is lucid, uncluttered, rather fluid, into passages that are clogged, wrenched, often tortured—a dizzying leap from diction that resembles sometimes Yeats and sometimes Auden to that suggesting, more than anyone else, Hopkins. The difference is largely one of compression (again looking toward *Mistress Bradstreet*), which, coupled with a jagged cacophony, sometimes makes for difficulties of interpretation. A few of the poems, notably "The Long Home" and "Narcissus Moving," are incomprehensible, largely because Berryman has

not yet honed the complex new language to his purposes. Others
("A Winter-Piece" and "The Dispossessed" for example) are uneven, the shifting language occasionally working brilliantly, sometimes remaining private and unduly obscure. Since these strange
poems help prepare the way for the later sequences, one welcomes them. Their value, however, is historical rather than aesthetic.

The book is made up of clusters of poems that have thematic
and stylistic coherence. I want to comment on a representative
poem or two from each section in order to isolate significant characteristics and to chart the movement from the early work to the
later. To begin with, the seven poems in Section I (including
"Winter Landscape" and "The Statue") are all characterized sty-
listically by the pellucid iambic pentameter line and thematically
by a preoccupation with permanence and loss. Echoes of Yeats,
Auden, and Pound are pervasive. Moreover, "The Traveller"
makes it clear that, although his *Stephen Crane* was not published until 1950, Berryman was already well immersed in that
poet's cosmic paranoia:

> They pointed me out on the highway, and they said
> 'That man has a curious way of holding his head.'
>
> They pointed me out on the beach; they said 'That man
> Will never become as we are, try as he can.'

This poem also introduces a symbolic journey motif that becomes
dominant in Section II.

The final two poems in the first section, both variations on the
theme of childhood loss, give evidence of serious tonal problems,
possibly because the poet was not yet able to deal effectively with
matters close to his own experience. "The Ball Poem" (vaguely
reminiscent of "Voyages II," in which Hart Crane watches children frisk on a beach and offers some avuncular advice) deals

with the loss of innocence, as symbolized in a boy's lost ball. The speaker, watching the boy, is sympathetic but playful, introducing a bawdy pun ("O there are other balls") and offering some bouncy alliterative wisdom: "People will take balls, / Balls will be lost always, little boy. / And no one buys a ball back." A few lines later, however, the tone shifts dramatically (and drastically) with the poet exploring "the deep and dark / Floor of the harbour." Suddenly, as always happens when anything is dark and deep, be it snowy woods or harbor, things become terribly mysterious and significant. Even more damaging, the paternal poet is immediately transformed into a Whitmanic pantheistic presence, and the poem collapses completely:

> . . . I am everywhere,
> I suffer and move, my mind and my heart move
> With all that move me, under the water
> Or whistling, I am not a little boy.

A clue to Berryman's inability to find and sustain a tone for dealing with loss is found in "Fare Well," addressed to the ghost of his father, "The eyes shadowed and shut." Here the dark and deep tone is appropriate, but the mood is undercut by Audenesque (or perhaps Hamletesque) word play, which reduces the terrible visitation to an occasion for cleverness: "What has been taken away will not return, / I take it." And worse, "After so long, can I long so and burn, / Imperishable son?" This is clearly a way of distancing material one finds too disturbing to face, but it makes for a schizophrenic poem. (When a Beckett character says something unsettling, he invariably undercuts it with an ironic reversal.) The deeply felt final lines ("Father I fought for Mother, sleep where you sleep") help recover the opening mood, but by then too much harm has been done. The lyric is too slight to bear the burden of the two modes, and the contradictory voices cancel each other out. It was to be many years before Berryman could come to terms, in his life and in his work, with his traumatic childhood loss.

The book's second section deals with "conclusions of the night," voyages in the dark, decay, and possession. The outer world is in a terrible state of chaos, and in the inner world a hectic fever constantly threatens to burn out of control. The poems, in fact, are punctuated with references to derangement, related to the idea of being possessed: "the vessels of my brain burst," "the overhead horror, in the padded room," "And like a hound he leapt out of his mind." Less dramatic but equally persistent are the references to horrors by night, fears, violence, dangerous shadows, nightmares, the moon of blood, the solitary dark. These images of night, of possession, and of horror all fuse to create passages that are interestingly fantastic but that never quite come into sharp focus.

Nearly all of Berryman's thoughts are related to night. Day, and particularly noon, remains a symbol of an unachievable ideal, a kind of Byzantium far removed from the dark world where man's mind conjures up spectres and where his animal self bites, breeds, and produces dung. For the most part the poems lack emotional resonance, so that the reader, while understanding the principle of possession, is unlikely, because the imagery is shadowy and the allusions historical rather than personal, to respond with any intensity. In the two best poems in the section, however, Berryman discovers metaphors through which he is able vividly, concretely, and evocatively (this last especially important since the power to evoke is most crucially lacking in the more cerebral early poems) to communicate his internal struggles. "World's Fair," in three beautifully wrought nine-line stanzas, presents the speaker as a solitary figure waiting, motionless, on a midway while fireworks burst over a lake and restless couples enter a roller-coaster to escape for a few moments a life they cannot understand. As he waits, the man's mind is nagged by an unformed idea which, in the central stanza, comes into focus:

Suddenly in torn images I trace
The inexhaustible ability of a man
Loved once, long lost, still to prevent my peace,
Still to suggest my dreams and starve horizon.
Childhood speaks to me in an austere face.
The Chast Mayd only to the thriving Swan
Looks back and back with lecherous intent,
Being the one nail known, an excrement;
Middleton's grave in a forgotten place.

The conjuring up of childhood in this carnival setting is artful and convincing. And the image of being possessed by the memory of a man who though long lost still has the power to prevent one's peace would be effective even if the lines lacked the resonance that comes from an awareness of Berryman's austere childhood. It is especially instructive to see how the poet, as he does in "Fare Well," immediately distances himself from this confrontation with his most disturbing knowledge. This time he shields himself not with wit, however, but with literary allusion, which moves him out of the chaotic world of immediate apprehension into the safer domain of art. The allusions, though obscure, are so apt that rather than undercut the moment of personal recognition they help focus it. As Margaret McBride has cogently pointed out, the references to the Chast Mayd and to the nail, both from Thomas Middleton's play *A Chaste Maid in Cheapside,* reinforce the idea of the poet as the means of his own self-destruction. At the same time, she adds, because the men *are* father and son, "their strong identification with and dependence upon each other twist their drive to destroy the enemy into deadly and inevitable self-destruction as well." [3] In the final stanza the speaker, "exhausted, angry," has now discovered the "track" that was lost in stanza one, and will return home further to confront "the instructor down my mind." The anguish, which so often in Berryman's early lyrics is generalized, diffuse, or ungrounded in experience, is communicated with a stunning specificity.

Even more powerful is the first version of "The Animal Trainer," a dialogue between mind and body reminiscent of Yeats's "The Circus Animals' Desertion," and also of "Sailing to Byzantium." The journey in these eight diminishing stanzas, however, is away from Byzantium, with its intellectual music, and toward the sensual movement, toward a full and, for the maturing Berryman, crucial acceptance of the foul rag-and-bone shop of the heart. The poem begins with an assertion of transience, "I must be gone" ("That is no country for old men"), but ends not with the image of an artificial bird upon a golden bough, but with the recognition of one's humanity: "You léarn from animals. You léarn in the dark." As the poem begins, the animal trainer (mind) talks of extricating himself from nature and the world of night to embody artistic purity in the "steady and exalted light of the sun." ("Leave me, O love, which reaches but to dust," Sidney wrote, "And thou, my mind, aspire to higher things.") Heart asks whether he can live without his animals,

> The looking, licking, smelling animals?
> The friendly fumbling beast? The listening one?
> That standing up and worst of animals?

These lines, suggesting the senses and the penis (the worst of animals), focus the nature of the trainer's plight:

> They plague me, they will not perform, they run
> Into forbidden corners, they fight, they steal.
> Better to live like an artist in the sun.

Heart eventually wins the debate, clinching his argument with the assertion that without the animals "No sun will save you." The poem ends without a definitive capitulation by the speaker, though the sense of the final lines is that he is willing to accept his animals, and the prospect of the night, and to learn from them. This somewhat ambiguous ending is more effective than that of the second version, which closes with too easy an acquiescence by the speaker, one that rather sentimentally rejects the not altogether negligible attractions of pure light: "Animals little and large, be still, be still: / I'll stay with you. Suburb and sun are pale."

Whatever their relative merit, these are important poems in the early Berryman canon; they represent a breakthrough of the most crucial sort, involving a willingness to let the senses play some part in his life as a poet. The humorless, abstract, often bloodless quality of much of the early work, inhibited even in an age of arid art, gives evidence of the price Berryman paid for rejecting the validity of his own sensory experience, for attempting to inhabit a suburb of noon as a way of dealing with a world of darkness. Only by accepting and learning from his own "animals" could he move beyond a cautious apprenticeship into his own tortured and exhilarating maturity.

The lessons Berryman was learning do not, unfortunately, find their fruition in the eight-poem sequence that immediately follows the animal trainer poems, but somewhat later. The third section is the bleakest in the book, its dominant themes being loss and crisis, its pervasive mood one of spiritual desolation. The landscape is a bitter and exhausted place out of which memory grows. The poems were written in the early forties, and (with the exception of "A Poem for Bhain") have war as either a central or peripheral subject. It is worth remembering that Berryman did not experience war, as Jarrell, Shapiro, or, in an odder way, Lowell did, and as a result his commentary smells of the lamp, has about it the bookishness of an editorial. These poems reinforce my conviction that Berryman succeeds less well with the social-ironic speculative poem, by way of Auden, than with the personal lyric, Yeatsian or not, that has its source in his own feelings.

The central difficulty with this work lies in the consistently stilted and wrenched character of the language, distorted not in a Hopkinsesque manner as a means of attaining a jagged compression, but in a way suggesting, again and again, that the concept is at the mercy of the form. The results are unidiomatic phrases, inversions, and language that is at times downright foolish:

> That afternoon a man squat' on the shore
> > "1 September, 1939"

> The history of strangers in their dreams
> Being irresponsible, is fun for men . . .
> > "Desire is a World by Night"

> Therefore the loud man, the man small and shy
> Who squats, the hostess, as she has a nut
> Laughing like ancestor . . .
> > "Farewell to Miles"

> > Who would feel
> Disdain, as she does, being put on show
> By whom she loves?
> > "The Enemies of the Angels"

I purposely avoid quoting from the *pièce de résistance* of the section, "Boston Common," an eighteen-stanza "Meditation upon the Hero," not because there are no examples of tortured language but because the poem as a whole is so crushingly dull that it would be unfair to discriminate against any of its lines by selecting only the most tedious.

After the labored speculations of this poetic cluster the three love poems and nine "Nervous Songs" of Section IV are especially welcome. The lyrics comprise a unit, "Canto Amor" describing a marriage eloquently ("more beautiful than midnight stars more frail"), and "The Lightning" playfully ("My love loves chocolate, she loves also me"), while "Surviving Love" documents the breakup of a marriage, the wife "gone brave & quick to her new life." "Canto Amor" bears comparison with such love lyrics as Williams' "Of Asphodel" and Ransom's "Winter Remembered." Berryman demonstrates absolute control of terza rima, transcending its technical restrictions to create an effect that is fluid and open. The tone is consistently affectionate without ever lapsing into sentimentality, and the diction is sharp, interestingly quirky rather than strained. The image patterns of light and darkness, heat and cold, storm and quiet, and of "new musics," are elegantly worked out and coalesce in a way that is engagingly solemn and luminously clear.

Two stanzas from the poem's invocation demonstrate the delicacy of Berryman's language, and show how close the poetry comes to the richness of *Mistress Bradstreet* at its most compressed:

> If (Unknown Majesty) I not confess
> praise for the wrack the rock the live sailor
> under the blue sea,—yet I may You bless
>
> always for hér, in fear & joy for hér
> whose gesture summons ever when I grieve
> me back and is my mage and minister.

There are several notable things about these lines. For one, this is the first time the poet has dropped the convention of capital letters at the beginning of all lines, not, to be sure, particularly significant, but indicative of a new openness, a greater flexibility. The introduction of the Hopkins diacritical marks and of the ampersand, both devices that were to harden into mannerism, give evidence of his developing assumption that a poem is to be seen as well as heard. The playful parenthetical address (reminiscent of Auden's "Sir, no man's enemy") brings in a note of serene levity altogether missing in the earlier work, the wit of which (such as it is) is arch rather than graceful. The telescoping of "I do not confess" to "I not confess" is the result not of a slavish adherence to the demands of the pentameter line (though the extra syllable would alter the rhythm) but of a desire to create a language that is both distinctive and fresh. The substitution of "ever when" for "whenever," again though it prevents rhythmical disruption, is motivated by the same purpose. The absence of the expected commas in the second line is another indication of a desire to work with optimum freedom within the tight constraints of a difficult form. And the archaic word "mage" (a magician, wizard), in addition to adding to the assonance of "praise" and "may," shows Berryman's predilection for spare and strange diction. Finally, the witty use of "minister," looking back as it does to "Unknown Majesty," typifies his ability to unify lines through effects that call little or no attention to themselves.

I want to quote the poem's conclusion, which further illustrates Berryman's exquisite lyricism and shows how far he has come toward the discovery of a unique style:

> Therefore the streaming torches in the grove
> through dark or bright, swiftly & now more near
> cherish a festival of anxious love.
>
> Dance for this music, Mistress to music dear,
> more, that storm worries the disordered wood
> grieving the midnight of my thirtieth year
>
> and only the trial of our music should
> still this irresolute air, only your voice
> spelling the tempest may compel our good:
>
> Sigh then beyond my song: whirl & rejoice!

The hovering and plunging joy of these stanzas exceptionally sings. Every detail (including "spelling," which looks back to "mage") has been elegantly prepared by the earlier stanzas. One is reminded that Berryman's final poem, published in *Delusions Etc.*, ends with a portrayal of King David dancing his "blue head off," but where this image, given the facts of the poet's death, takes on an ominous note, the conclusion of "Canto Amor" is one of unclouded liberation.

In the other major achievement of *The Dispossessed,* the sequence of nervous songs, Berryman for the first time adopts the dramatic mode. The nine soliloquies are spoken by an odd collection of men and women who seem on the surface to have little in common but who are actually variations on a single type. They are solitary figures, and all are slightly (or not so slightly) neurotic, agitated, living on the edge of breakdown, confused, tormented, obsessed. Their songs are "nervous" in that they express emotional tension, restlessness, agitation—a disordered state of the nerves. Each speaker is in a moment of crisis of one sort or another (or has passed beyond into madness), and the responses to the hectic agitation involve, in virtually every case, a form of paranoia, an obsession with the uncontrollable elements (especially fire and water), and, either latent or recognized, a deep-rooted death wish. Though some are more effective than others, the nine poems stand as a compelling series of psychological studies. In its form, the three six-line stanzas with flexible rhyme schemes, and in its mood of intense auto-revelation, the sequence is an important forerunner of *The Dream Songs.*

The first song, that of a young woman, is a somewhat obscure, slightly ambiguous, but nevertheless powerful expression of self-loathing and sexual frustration. As this female Prufrock lies in her bath, thinking of her body as a bobbing cork and yearning for a penis ("I want something to hang to"), her mind drifts over the details by which she has measured out her life—a little vague chat, a £3.10 hat. Utterly self-involved (the pronoun "I" appears fifteen times), she longs for a transcendent experience, a losing of herself, perhaps in erotic experience (the full moon), perhaps in death. The movement from the cork and bath to the image of being "lifted lost in the flood" measures the distance between her reality and her fantasy, and though unlike Prufrock she insists "I am not afraid," one gathers that her nervous confusion is the result of her inhibition.

The second poem is a diabolical song of paranoid confusion sung by a demented priest who is at the mercy of the elements, and who regards himself, in an explicit death wish, as "king" of the dead. His is a textbook case of persecution ("Someone inter-feres / Everywhere with me"), and while the young woman's world is grounded in real bathtubs and real hats, the priest in-habits an hallucinatory country in which God communicates with him and where legions of the dead dance. By contrast, the young Hawaiian of the third song, though part of a decaying world and of a dying race, seems to inhabit a palpable world of sensuous girls, green palms, and creaming surf. This young man, randy and ripe in his phallic prime, this king of the living who will not take only one girl but will "dance them all," seems very much out of place in this raddled company. The illusion is collapsed, how-ever, as we see him swimming from the black sand at noon, swimming farther than the others, "for I swim alone, / . . . (Whom Nangganangga smashed to pieces on / The road to Para-dise.)" Primitive societies do not take kindly to bachelorhood—in Hawaiian mythology the god Nangganangga stands on the road to Paradise smashing with a club any unmarried male who tries to get past him. The young Hawaiian, it turns out, is king only of the dead.

The Professor's song also takes place at noon, and though couched in witty couplets as a manic lecture to a bored class, it clearly represents the internal musing of a man at the end of his tether. Beginning in medias res "(. . rabid or dog-dull)" the speaker proceeds by a process of pedantic jokes ("Troll me," "Fished out"), dry epistemology ("the world is from the French"), intellectual disdain ("Squint soon," "red all your eyes"), and liter-ary allusions (Blake, "deep romantic chasm," Mozart) to his funny and mad conclusion, which resolves the rabies image of the opening: "Until I meet you, then, in Upper Hell / Convulsed, foaming immortal blood: farewell." In its wit and mania the song is considerably more appealing than the predictable "Jocks-and-blondes-in-Chaucer-303" that turn up with such regularity in academic journals.

"The Captain's Song" finds its source in *Moby-Dick*. The speaker has forsaken domesticity to seek a mystical revelation, which comes to him when the mast of the ship blooms into flame, the tongues of fire falling above him like blood. In the second stanza, calm after the violence of the first, he experiences sorrow's crown of sorrow, remembering his vigorous childhood when he outran everyone and, like the Young Hawaiian, "darted off alone." This imagery sets up the third stanza in which, planning his return, he remembers how on cold nights he warmed his wife's feet with both of his, and he asks "Will I warm her with one?" This is the only song in which the slightly mad aspect of a speaker is coupled with physical disability. Although conveying a good deal of power, the poem, after the robust fireworks of the opening, is rather more slack and simple than the others. No reading, moreover, is quite so affecting as the first, since the impact depends for the most part on the shock ending.

The sixth poem, modelled on Yeats's "Crazy Jane" sequence, is called "The Song of the Tortured Girl," and this time the pain is not wholly self-inflicted. This song, Berryman said in an interview, is about a heroine of the French Resistance "captured by the Gestapo, and tortured, in various ways, to death, *without giving up any names.*" [4] (The poem, interestingly, predates the McCarthy witch hunts.) There is nothing in early Berryman that surpasses the disoriented inevitability and imaginative logic of "And there were sudden noises, which I made." The brutalized girl, on the verge of death, could be a heroic version of the young woman in the first song. In that poem, however, "A fierce wind" roared in a bare tree, and now that power has been diminished by the speaker's confused state: "Through leafless branches the sweet wind blows / Making a mild sound, softer than a moan." Like the Captain, the girl remembers a better time, a moment of transcendent delight: "High in a pass once where we put our tent, / Minutes I lay awake to hear my joy." This emotion recollected in desolation is remarkably like that of the dream songs ("Once in a sycamore I was glad"), which document a pervasive sense of loss; the tortured girl is a spiritual forerunner of poor, confused Henry House.

In the final three songs the death wish is dominant. "The Song of the Bridegroom," in some ways the oddest and most obscure of the group, presents a Prufrockian sensibility paralyzed by sexual fears and by a terror of the brutal forms "beating eyes upon my window." Unlike the Hawaiian, who wants to dance all of the girls, the bridegroom wants nothing so much as to be laid away, like a piece of crystal, "Felted in depths of caves, dark cupboards that / No one would open for a long time." Desolate, frightened, and exhausted, he nevertheless stoically accepts the responsibilities of continuing life, of entering the door that brought him forth: "I extend my hand and place it in the womb." The images—crystal, ceremonial fire, the journey home—never coalesce, and as a result this poem is less disturbing than the others.

The "Song of the Man Forsaken and Obsessed," spoken by an immobilized painter, probably Gauguin, lying in a hut in a strange land, is a plea to be freed from his "decayed feet, cock and heart" and to exist as pure brain "with a little vermilion!" The song's vitality derives from the vigorous manner in which the painter describes his preoccupation with the dissolution of his animal self: "My nails and my hair loosen / The stiff flesh lurches and flows off like blood." The poem is artistically unified, or composed, like a still life, the image of vermilion beginning and resolving its tensions. A line is dropped from the final stanza, thus reinforcing the general theme of decay and diminution.

In the final song not only is no line dropped, but the three stanzas are worked out in a highly formal rhyme scheme, abcabc. Like the other personae in the sequence, the speaker is tortured, this time by the horror of human bloodshed. He is possessed by dreams of those who have been murdered, "Bearded with woe, their eyes blasted and dull." Earth's citizen, he is able to avoid participation in actual wars (thus provoking his country's wrath), but is unable to escape the internal violence that is an inevitable part of the experience of being human:

> What I try, doomed, is hard enough to do.
> We breed up in our own breast our worse wars
> Who long since sealed ourselves Hers Who abides.

The penultimate line could serve as an epigraph for the whole sequence, since though the speakers are storm-buffeted and flame-singed, it is the demons within that are largely responsible for the anguish.

There is nothing in the final section of *The Dispossessed* that begins to match the energy and incandescent reality of these songs. One reads with a sense of disappointment and anticlimax; only one poem, "New Year's Eve," has any real merit. Composed in eight stanzas consisting of an abab opening followed by two couplets, it documents—in its doggerel double rhymes, its ironies, and its imagery—the pervasive influence of Eliot and Auden. The work contains a poem within a poem. The frame is conventional cocktail party verse, replete with the inevitable acrid air, whisky, banal chatter, and adulterous flirtations. In the third stanza the speaker, slightly juiced, launches into a monologue on artists, asking (and answering) "Why it is our promise breaks in pieces early." Combining imagery of politics and po-

etics, the poet sees himself as a linsey-woolsey workman, grandi-
ose and slack, and as a priest of the infinite. The section ends
"Our tools in; / brownshirt Time chiefly our works will burn."
This is followed by a memory passage, a radiant picture of physical labor that stands, compared to the vagaries of artistic creation,
as a kind of noble ideal. The stanza is one of Berryman's most
memorable.

In the final stanza that poet returns to the party, announcing
the arrival of the New Year, "my Retarded One." He makes his
peace with the dying dragon, "Worst of Years," now exorcized
(dispossession once again), and clasps upon the stroke, "kissing
with happy cries." The poem is remarkable partly because it tran-
scends the conventions of satirical cocktail party verse, largely
through the balancing of the real and the ideal, and partly because it has such an obvious bearing on Berryman's own experience. The dying dragon is 1947, and it was in this worst of years
that the poet, faced with a suicidal depression over his inability to
persuade his mistress to leave her husband, turned to psycho-
therapy as a way of dealing with his demons. The poem represents a point of delicate balance, an acceptance of the validity of
the past and a cautious greeting of the future, which arrives
stamping off freezing slush, scotch under his arm. If the aesthetic
theorizing threatens to throw the poem utterly out of focus, the
work nevertheless succeeds, not brilliantly but well, in recording
a crucial time in the poet's life. The more dazzling lyrics were
still to come.

CHAPTER 2

The Princeton Mistress

"I began work in verse-making
as a burning, trivial disciple
of the great Irish poet William
Butler Yeats, and I hope I have
moved off from there."

When his sonnets were published in 1967, twenty years after
they were composed, Berryman added a preface, in the dream
song stanza, in which he announces that the songs were made "A
THOUSAND YEARS AGO," and that after some indecision
about whether to destroy them he has decided to "FREE THEM
TO THE WINDS THAT PLAY." [1] Having achieved some emotional distance from the events they describe he was able, or
nearly able, to regard these poems as historical artifacts with little
relevance to his present self. And it would be possible for a
reader to see them as rather quaint valentines from another time
except that their euphoria and pain are so genuine, their rhythms
so seductive, and their imagery so vivid that one is likely to be
drawn into the passionate world they depict. The 115 poems are
the record of a stormy "knock-down-drag-out love," and as such

they represent, in their confessional intensity and personal imagery, a major departure from the work of *The Dispossessed*.

On a first reading, or perhaps after several, the sequence may seem to be somewhat inaccessible, slightly obscure, too private to communicate generally. The poems, after all, were composed as a personal journal, or, perhaps, as love letters to a woman called "Lise," and they contain numerous allusions that seem to be impenetrable. Moreover, drawing as they do on the conventions of the sonnet sequence, the lyrics, for all their personal revelations, are extraordinarily literary, thickly allusive, filled with echoes. And the diction is odd (frequently very odd), with esoteric and archaic words (and even nonwords) proliferating and suggesting difficulties that are, in fact, more imaginary than real. Once one reads through the book two or three times the difficulties largely disappear, and though there are lines that refuse to yield to a rigorous analysis the sequence as a whole, with its recurring images, characters, places, and emotions, emerges as nearly transparent. There are hints here and there that the poet, like many a diarist before him, had the wider public at least in the back of his mind as he wrote, and that he was as aware of literary convention as he was of his own personal need to put words around the feelings he was experiencing during the most erotically intense period of his life.

The sequence begins with a reference to a time, in middle March, before the relationship between the poet and his Lady had been consummated. The final sonnet suggests the affair's conclusion. With the weather changing, the poet waits, in their usual trysting place, for Lise, who does not come: "I sat down & wrote." The poems in between describe an adulterous relationship, stormy and work-destroying, that takes place during the summer of 1946, an affair interrupted by Lise's absences from Princeton, and finally completed (though this does not appear in the work) by her unwillingness to divorce her husband. The sonnets record the poet's passion, preoccupation, despair, and guilt during these months of lies and love.

The reference to "middle March" in the opening sonnet suggests George Eliot's novel, with its middle-aged scholar and his vivacious young wife. Berryman, however, is clearly no Casaubon. He is, rather, a vigorous 32-year-old man living in Princeton and working, or (as the poem makes clear) not working, on a long poem. He is married to "Esther," a minimal disguise for Eileen. Lise, "the topaz woman," the subject and object of his poems, is revealed largely in terms of his responses to her. We do, however, pick up a good many concrete details along the way. She is 27, blonde, has gray-blue eyes, and is "breasty." She is married to "David," who apparently has a personality much less powerful than hers, and they have a young son named Peter. Lise plays the harpsichord, is enthusiastic about classical music, and is not keen on poetry. She is, like the poet, from Oklahoma, the daughter of an oil man. Also like the poet, she was born under the sign of Scorpio. Vivacious, reckless, and highstrung, she drinks a blue streak. These various details, plus numerous images relating to shining, blazing, and flaming, suggest a woman who is independent, forthright, secure, and disturbingly attractive.

The strength and confidence of Lise are amusingly counterpoised against the characteristics of the poet, who adopts the conventional role of wan and pale lover, and who, in the face of his erotic yearnings, his mistress' occasional cruelty, his jealousy, and his role as hypocritical adulterer, emerges as a slightly ridiculous figure, a slave to love, at times almost a fool. The quasimasochistic suffering and the self-effacement both derive from the Petrarchian convention, as reinforced by Wyatt and Surrey. But so pervasive is the imagery of buffoonery and so powerful the sense of self-hatred that these things assume an absolutely central position, the odd loss of self-esteem becoming at times more absorbing than anything else in the sequence. The allusions to the poet's sense of himself reveal just how totally the affair has annihilated his usually powerful machismo as well as his general habit of dominating any love relationship. He refers to himself as martyr, fool, victim, acolyte, pale ridiculous thing, slave, clown, ghost, and swine-enchanted lover. He likens himself to a loon, a blind child, an ass, a parasite, a stone, a moth, and to a burnt offering. He is the "penal colony's prime scribe" and "the officer flat on my own machine." He is tame, lame, bizarre, astonished, lone & wild, frantic, and "this strange thing I despised." He is, in short, utterly in the thrall of the reckless lady, "blonde, barefoot, beautiful," who, never subjected to the same sort of caricature, is always described in variations of "sunlight vollying down the blue air," always seen as an object worthy of worship. If the contrast between the two seems at times absurd, it helps explain the odd language in which the passion is communicated, and provides an intriguing preview of a later narrator, the comical, self-deprecating Henry of the *Songs*.

It would be misleading, of course, to suggest that the principal emotion communicated by the sonnets is that conveyed by the poet's often obsequious idolatry, or to imply that the power of the poetry can be communicated in terms of its paraphrasable content. Berryman manages, in spite of his speaker's comic self-deflations, to give many of the poems a tone of high seriousness. Since the sequence charts the emotions of a complex summer, we are moved from passages in which verbal wit and levity, a kind of good-natured playfulness, create the dominant mood, to those in which the colors darken to the point of a despair bordering on the suicidal: "I am dreaming of the hour when I can hear / My last lie rattle, and then lie truly still." Berryman may be no more Melpomene's, but Erato's fool, that is, the subject of the muse of love poetry rather than of tragedy, but he is still capable of creating effects that can move the reader to pity and fear.

As in any sequence the effect of individual poems is enhanced when they are seen in relation to one another, even though all are self-contained. One source of this cumulative richness lies in the frequent variations on certain images, each repetition tying the poem, by subtle strands, to all the others with which it shares details. One such image pattern is a wind-rain-storm cluster similar to that by which Berryman achieves atmospheric effects in his earlier lyrics. The sonnets are filled with thunder, cold rain, hurricane, storms, and lightning-flash. These natural phenomena have little to do with the climate of Princeton, much to do with the quality of the cyclonic love affair, strikingly different from the relatively calm relationships between the poet and Esther and between Lise and David. These weather images function as objective correlative, evoking an inner climate that has little in common with the much-annotated mental state suggested by a patient etherized upon a table.

An even more pervasive pattern derives from the traditional association of love and fire, on which it works numerous variations, many of the poems employing images of heat-cold, flame, fire, burning, burnt offerings, and blazing, which delineate the sexual dimension of the affair: "I burn . . . am led / Burning to slaughter." Lise is invariably linked with sunlight, gold, shining, and white flame, emerging as a golden girl responsible for the poet's algolagnia, the pleasing pains associated with burning in her blazing power: "I am the sky / Vehicle of your cadmium shine . . . your choir."

> . . . but darling you are sunlight
> Volleying down blue air, waking a flight
> Of sighs to follow like the morning iris
> Your shining-out-of-shadow hair . . .

While these variations on fire and storm reappear throughout the book, there are numerous sonnets in which Berryman (like his master in "When to the sessions of sweet silent thought," to choose an obvious example) plays and puns on one or more images, often with witty and ingenious results. Sonnet 59, for example, discreetly but nevertheless bawdily plays on the theme of fellatio, linking such words as sucks, blown, charming loss, harden, come. Number 71, "Our Sunday morning," fuses ecclesiastical and erotic imagery, and winningly quotes a phrase from Stevens' "Sunday Morning." Number 73 draws its images from Kafka, #109 from "Tristan and Isolde," #15 from Petrarch, #25 from navigation, #81 from physics, #97 from magic and warfare. Number 51 is perhaps the most calculated in its effects, playing on an aviary theme with words such as trills, prinks, bill, flew, dart, philomel, and even introducing a catalpa tree, the literal meaning of catalpa being "head with wings." This sort of cleverness can cloy if it becomes mannered, but in the case of the sonnets Berryman has studied his several sources with discretion, and his variations are presented, invariably, in a manner that is crafty rather than self-indulgent.

A sense of place contributes another unifying factor to the book's disparate parts. There are two major settings, one of which, appearing in a score or so of the poems, is the pine grove ("the nave of pines") just outside town, where the lovers meet early in the morning. The other setting is the town of Princeton, whose institution of higher learning is referred to with benign good humor by the Columbia-educated poet as "The University of Soft Knocks." At one point, playing on the University's mascot, he likens the sleeping town to a toothless tiger:

> Nothing the borough lets be made here, lest
> The professors and the millionaires from bed
> Be startled, the Negroes drop trays, build.

One detail within the Princeton setting is especially worth noting. This is a sycamore tree in front of Lise's stone home, mentioned once in mock-jealousy, because it "More than I see you sees you," and again when the poet climbs it: "Hand trembling on the top, everything was / Beautiful, inhuman, green and real as usual." The lines almost certainly foreshadow an important moment in the first *Dream Song:*

> Once in a sycamore I was glad
> all at the top, and I sang.
> Hard on the land wears the strong sea
> and empty grows every bed.

(Another probable source for these lines is Delmore Schwartz: "High in the summer branches the poet sang. / His throat ached, and he could sing no more.") It is tempting to connect the sense of despair, the "departure" that opens the *Songs,* with Princeton, and to suggest that the end of the affair with Lise was a kind of exile from the only Eden the poet ever knew.

Much of the verbal texture of the poems is created by quirky, archaic, and obscure words. These give the book a slightly exotic and antiquarian quality, and will pose problems to any reader, however erudite, not willing to make frequent pilgrimages to a good dictionary. Widely read and in love with language, Berryman, like Stevens, took delight in spare, odd-sounding, out-of-the-way language, and some sublime rarities show up in these songs: mome, loblolly, dinch, nixe, hircine, utraquist, keek, tors, jerquer, aits, scrutators. The list could go on.

The sonnets are nearly all in the Petrarchan, or Italian, form. A typical poem consists of an octave, generally raising an issue or posing a question, and rhyming abba abba, or some variation on this, plus a sestet, providing some sort of resolution, and rhyming typically cde cde. The rhythm is iambic pentameter. In all but a score or so there is a space between the octave and sestet, suggesting a major break. In most of these, moreover, the octave is end-stopped and the thought complete. In a number of the poems there is no division between the parts, save that created by rhyme patterns, and in these, typically, there is no end stop following the eighth line. In three poems (14, 47, 54) both the octave and sestet are divided in half by blank space, thus creating four discrete parts. Berryman takes very few liberties with meter; the pentameter is regular as clockwork. On several occasions, however, he adds from two to four feet to the final line, in some cases creating what is in effect a fifteenth line. His insistence on regular metrics occasionally forces him into awkward phrasing, in which the sense is clearly at the mercy of the syllable count, as in "But not this: what a bastard, not spring wide" (number 7), or "Nothing there? Nothing up the sky alive" (number 35). Generally, however, the lines, though rigidly controlled, give the impression of a good deal of freedom and fluidity.

In order to give a full sense of Berryman's line, as well as of his general approach to syntax and diction, I want to comment on two representative poems. First, number 13:

> I lift—lift you five States away your glass,
> Wide of this bar you never graced, where none
> Ever I know came, where what work is done
> Even by these men I know not, where a brass
> Police-car sign peers in, wet strange cars pass,
> Soiled hangs the rag of day out over this town,
> A juke-box brains air where I drink alone,
> The spruce barkeep sports a toupee alas—
>
> My glass I lift at six o'clock, my darling,
> As you plotted . . Chinese couples shift in bed,
> We shared today not even filthy weather,
> Beasts in the hills their tigerish love are snarling,
> Suddenly they clash, I blow my short ash red,
> Grey eyes light! and we have our drink together.

This is one of several sonnets written during Lise's absence. These tend to be among the most effective and most deeply felt, probably because the separation provided some perspective and a kind of emotional calm not possible during the turbulent days when the two were together. Here the lovers achieve a moment of long-distance communication by toasting each other at an agreed-upon hour. The charm of the poem lies in the contrast between the tawdry details relating to the bar and the luminous image of Lise, whose eyes are conjured up in the final line. The octave gives the local setting, with the poet's isolation (and alienation) expressed by the unknown men, the "wet strange cars," the soiled rag of day, the juke-box, and the spruce barkeep. The effect is one of slightly inhospitable seediness, an ideal setting for anonymous brooding and drinking. The most telling image of the section is in the comic final line with its reference to the toupee. Like the soiled rag hanging over the town, the artificial hair helps evoke a world of faintly murky surreality. Though all of the details are presented with benign good humor, a stale atmosphere of decay nevertheless pervades the lines.

In the sestet the poem opens up from the safe inside world of a bar to the passionate world beyond where Chinese couples make love and where beasts clash and couple. The poet's small, private gesture of lust, blowing the ash of his cigarette red, is to passion what the toupee is to hair, yet it manages to conjure the image of his mistress—he has now retreated within himself away from police-cars and juke-boxes, and experiences a moment of private communication. The poem gains its effects through the hard specificity of the several details, through the rendering of the two worlds—the alien, lifeless bar and the exotic hills where beasts snarl and clash—and through its simple diction and seductive rhythms. The "toast" is expressed in one flowing sentence, slowed but not stopped by the commas and dash. The double rhymes of the sestet teeter on the brink of doggerel and give the conclusion its rather whimsical and gentle tone. This is, in all, a charming poem, appealing in its expression of affection and vulnerability.

Number 41, a kind of inverse aubade, also describes the emotions associated with absence. This time, however, the mellow, slightly boozy late afternoon is replaced by the agitated staccato images of early morning depression:

> And Plough-month peters out . . its thermal power
> Squandered in sighs and poems and hopeless thought,
> Which corn and honey, wine, soap, wax, oil ought
> Upon my farmling to have chivvied into flower.
> I burn, not silly with remorse, in sour
> Flat heat of the dying month I stretch out taut:
> Twenty-four dawns the topaz woman wrought
> To smile to me is gone. These days devour
> Memory: what were you elbowed on your side?
> Supine, your knee flexed? do I hear your words
> Faint as a nixe, in our grove, saying farewells? . .
> At five I get up sleepless to decide
> What I will not today do; ride out: hear birds
> Antiphonal at the dayspring, and nothing else.

This is obviously a more complex lyric, the feelings of guilt and desolation requiring more complicated imagery than does a sense of bittersweet loneliness. The first quatrain introduces a theme that appears in several of the sonnets, in references such as "Work-destroying love," and "my work's broken down." Like all writers, Berryman experienced profound uneasiness when not able to work; he uses an agricultural image to suggest all of the practical necessities he should have produced—corn, soap, oil— during the hot Plough-month he has squandered. The thermal motif is continued in the second quatrain in the Hopkinsesque image of the poet stretched out tense and sour during a dark morning. Then the sense of loss is picked up in reference to days without the topaz woman devouring memory, so that even the images and words are lost. The final three lines describe, as well as any poet ever has, the stoical recognition of one's own loss of creative volition: to decide what I will not today do. The birds are singing their antiphonal music in the grove, the lovers' trysting place, and their hymn at dayspring is in bitter contrast to the poet's own depressed state. The poem succeeds because it communicates so painfully the speaker's sense of failure and desolation. The palpable reality of honey, wine, soap, and birdsong help put his vague inertia into focus. The sonnet, in its tone, verbal wit, and sharp revelation of a barren inner landscape, has many of the qualities one finds in *The Dream Songs*.

The poems written during Lise's absence comprise a self-contained group within the larger sequence. There are other clusters as well, though less significant in the comprehensive scheme. Several passages are about the sonnets themselves, focusing on the fact that they crowd out other work, and that they are meant only for Lise and will lack a larger audience. A few excerpts reveal the theme's characteristics:

> They may suppose, because I would not cloy your ear—
> If ever these songs by other ears are heard—
>
> #23

> They come too thick, hail-hard, and all beside
> Batter, necessities of my nights and days,
> My proper labour that my storm betrays
> Weekly lamented, weakly flung aside;
>
> #50

> Languid the songs I wish I willed . . I try . .
>
> #61

> Is it possible, poor kids, you must not come out?
> Care you for none but Lise, to whom you cry?
> Here in my small book you dance, then die?
> Rain nor sun greet you first, no friendly shout?
>
> #87

Another recurring theme has to do with the poet's wife and Lise's husband. Why can't they, the speaker asks, fall in love with each other? David emerges as more or less oblivious to the situation. Esther, however, is aware, and "suspects, drooping and vaguely sore, / Something entirely sad, skew, she not seeks." At one point Esther is described as "the sharer I desired," toward whom "I sailed back," but now that sailing "yaws." Lies and passion "sing in the cabin on the voyage home." The most explicit description of his anguish over hurting his wife, coupled with the inability to prevent himself from doing so, is found in number 69:

> For you am I collared O to quit my dear
> My sandy-haired mild good and most beautiful
> Most helpless and devoted wife? I pull
> Crazy away from this; but too from her
> Resistlessly I draw off, months have, far
> And quarrelling—irrelation—numb and dull
> Dead Sea with tiny aits . . Love at the full
> Had wavered, seeing, foresuffering us here.

He is aware that he "should have stuck with his own mate-O," but when he attempts to approach her, "the horror and beauty" of Lise's eyes burn between (83). The pain he is giving Esther, his despair over being unable to work, and the strength and mastery of Lise account for the occasionally comic but more often dark sense of self-loathing that permeates the book.

Since the sonnets contain patterns of recurring imagery, themes, characters, and settings, there is a temptation to find in the sequence a carefully worked out organizational plan. Any such strategy, however, would be in the mind of the reader rather than of the poet. The poems are diary entries (and love letters) chronicling events and emotions over which the poet has little control.. They chart a love affair over a period of several months, and as such the highs and lows are determined by the course of the relationship rather than by the exigencies of literary form. There is a gently unobtrusive temporal framework, worth noticing but not, ultimately, terribly important. The book begins, as I have mentioned, in "middle March," before the affair has been consummated. (Lise is likened to a cool mirage seen by a parched traveler.) The sequence is composed, we learn from internal details, during the months from May through August, though there is usually no way of knowing, sonnet by sonnet, when each takes place. A very crude framework can be pieced together from explicit evidence: number 9, for example, refers to Mayday, number 70 mentions May 3 as the day "we begin to fuse," number 53 mentions the "third day of July," number 74 is dated 18 July, and so forth. The final poem suggests both the end of the affair and the end of summer: "The weather's changing. This morning was cold. . . ."

This is all quite neat and, in a gross way, aesthetically satisfying. The affair begins in spring, and continues through a hot Princeton summer, nurtured by rainstorms and bright sunlight, finally to wither as fall approaches. The ordering of the sonnets is determined by chronology. Within this broad framework, however, there are smaller, less dramatic rhythms that are more significant insofar as the overall movement of the book is concerned. These, determined by the poet's internal seasons, are expressed by ascents and descents, by passages communicating comic self-ridicule followed by those expressing bleak despair, by descriptions of sexual passion giving way to feelings of guilt and confusion, by poems that are personal and colloquial fusing with those that are formal and allusive. These smaller cycles within the larger scheme delineate the chaos and occasional well-being experienced during the months of emotional upheaval, and they provide a more intense account of the affair's dimensions than does the predictable and orderly movement toward winter.

Since the poems were, apparently, written in the order in which they appear, there are occasionally illuminating transitions and continuations, as one sonnet picks up an image, or carries forward a dialogue, or suggests a response to the poem that precedes it. (These connections are in addition to the patterns by which works in the sequence are related to one another by the elaborate network of associations.) For example, the sonnet (number 4) in which Berryman describes himself as "no more Melpomene's, but Erato's fool," is followed by a description of visits he made while Melpomene's "monk" to T. S. Eliot ("The poet hunched, so, whom the worlds admire") and to Yeats, who "muttered before an Athenaeum fire." Number 6, in which the misery of waiting evokes a quietly disturbing death wish, is followed by an analysis of a suicide: "I said a man, life in his teeth, could care / Not much just whom he spat it on. . . ." Number 30 describes a car ride taken by the two couples, in which the poet plays the role of "the friendly joker," and this is followed by a more solemn commentary on the wickedness of "masks" and "lies." Numbers 33, 34, and 35 all play the theme of personal, legal, and holy laws. Number 44, a subtle variation on Donne's "but don't deny I love" is followed in 45 by specific reference to other Donne lines.

The final four poems also form a small, unified section, serving, after the erotic intensities that make up most of the book, to bring the sequence to a gentle conclusion. In number 112 a note of fatigue replaces the manic-depressive extremes, and with the phrases "You loom less," and "before I abandon you," the speaker suggests that the roaring fire is all but burned out. The next poem contains the word "Tetélestai," which indicates beyond any question that the affair is over. The word, spoken by Christ on the cross ("It is finished"), is used ritually, either in marriage or in death, to suggest both an end and a beginning: it is consummated. The physical relationship has ended, and the new time has begun, suggested in number 114, when the *idea* or memory of Lise "will come for years, above below, / & through to interrupt my study." In the final poem the transformation of Lise from woman to muse is completed. Earlier in the affair when she fails to appear in the grove the poet's response is despair: "I crush a cigarette black, and go down" (64). At the end of number 115 we see that the experience of the liaison is the source of creative energy, more important to the poet, perhaps, than is the relationship itself:

> The weather's changing. This morning was cold,
> as I made for the grove, without expectation,
> some hundred Sonnets in my pocket, old,
> to read her if she came. Presently the sun
> yellowed the pines & my lady came not
> in blue jeans & a sweater. I sat down & wrote.

Tetélestai. And this seems to be a response to the question raised in the introductory poem: "THE ORIGINAL FAULT WAS WHETHER WICKEDNESS / WAS SOLUBLE IN ART."

If the answer to this question lies largely in the quality of the art, what can be said, finally, about the sequence as a whole? For one thing, it is important in the development of Berryman's craft because for the first time, in any really substantial way, he drops the mask of neutral objectivity, abandons the cool, slightly exhausted and more than slightly derivative voice, and emerges as a unique man who records his own sensibility in a voice that, at least in the strongest, truest sonnets, is recognizably his own. It was essential, if Berryman was to break through from apprenticeship to mastery of his own talents, that he make the sort of commitment he describes in number 47:

> Double I sing, I must, your utraquist,
> Crumpling a syntax at a sudden need,
> Stridor of English softening to plead
> O to you plainly lest you more resist.

It took a theme that appealed to his deepest needs to bring Berryman to the necessity of "crumpling a syntax," to transform an empty monk of the Yeatsian order into love's utraquist, one who speaks or writes two languages, such as Latin and the vernacular. It is the experiments with colloquial language, slangy, often inelegant, hot off the heart, going directly to a feeling without attempting to sublime it into formal art, that give this book of utterly conventional structures its unconventional power and importance.

However, there was a side of Berryman, aged 32 in 1946, that was completely content with the connotations of his masters, capable of falling into the easy and characterless formal mode, the Latin without the vernacular. The fact that in an era in which Pound and Williams were exerting their liberating influence he chose to walk in the well-worn footsteps of Petrarch, Sidney, and Shakespeare, to name only the most obvious of his models, makes it clear that though his language is fresh, his poetics are conservative, his desire to master his craft transcending any need to make it new. And what more charming way, after all, to pay tribute to a dazzling mistress than by placing her in the company of Laura, and Stella, and the dark lady? How could one better honor his mistress than by making her the topaz lady of the sonnets?

The danger of adapting to a convention, of course, is that one can easily become merely conventional. Given the formal demands of a rigid rhyme scheme and an iambic pentameter line, plus the inherited burden of hundreds of years of quintessential mastery, how is one to avoid sounding like a grandfather clock imitating a great-grandfather clock? At their least impressive the sonnets do sound as if they may have been written by a committee—mannered, predictably regular, at the mercy of the form, verbally undistinguished and indistinctive. One can out-Wyatt Wyatt, but only at the risk of sounding like Wyatt. But because the experience he was documenting was itself so overwhelmingly new—all lovers are similar, but no two loves are even remotely alike—Berryman wrote from his own being, fleshing out the inherited sonnet skeleton with language that is peculiarly his own. One is reminded of Cummings, who wrote sonnets that appear on the surface to be eccentric but that are actually more conventional than the models from which they seem to deviate. Berryman, conversely, makes no attempt to disguise his form, yet by crumpling syntax in his own way, by finding words and images that mirror his own sensibility, and by daring to reveal aspects of himself generally considered to be too intimate even for lyric poetry, he manges, in a surprisingly large number of the poems, to fuse "jitterbug and pavanne," to create "a verse fresh as a bubble breaks." The seeds of the so-called confessional mode can clearly be discovered in these poems. Much of their quirky strength and odd appeal derive from the sort of vulnerability that makes it necessary for their creator to play games with himself, to adopt masks as a way of separating himself—and Lise—from some of his darker, perhaps even weaker, personal qualities, though these are invariably revealed:

> Burnt cork, my leer, my Groucho crouch and rush,
> No more my nature than Cyrano's: we
> Are 'hindered characters'
>
> # 100

The implication, simplistic but irresistible, is of a clown who laughs to conceal his broken heart. Like Cyrano, whose soul is noble but who nevertheless must play the buffoon, the poet is unable to make known his passion, and so puts on a comic mask to deflect attention from his true feelings. Like the family in Pirandello's *Six Characters in Search of an Author* he too is "hindered," not because his role has been left uncompleted but because his true role, as lover, is one he is forbidden to play, except in the privacy of his grove or of his study. The "burnt cork" looks suggestively toward Henry, another hindered character who plays in blackface, partly as a means of identifying with a persecuted race and partly as a way of concealing his own face and, by extension, his nature.

So the voices—the formal and the vernacular—alternate, respond to each other, together suggesting the nature of the speaker in ways neither could do by itself. The careful, stately lines, grievous and sublime, would be impressive but ultimately dull without the nervous interruptions of the Groucho mode— the puns, bawdy jokes, word play, self-deflating epithets, outlandish diction, personal anecdotes. If the sequence suffers from this slightly schizophrenic behavior it is not because the voices interrupt each other too often, but because they do not do so often enough. *The Dream Songs* is an eccentric masterpiece precisely because the vernacular mode is given full play, the exuberant persona permitted totally to crowd out the more conventional aspects of his sensibility when there are reasons for this to happen. In the *Sonnets* the disreputable side of the lover is still held in check; it threatens on occasion to burst forth in all its inventive vitality, but Berryman was not yet quite prepared to run the risks of such public behavior. That would come later.

CHAPTER 3

A New England Mistress

In a funeral elegy to Anne Bradstreet printed in the 1678 edition of her poems, John Norton wrote "time will a poet raise / Born under better Stars, shall sing thy praise." [1] That the stars under which Berryman was born were better than any others is at best doubtful, but that he honored Anne Bradstreet as few poets have ever done honor to another is indisputable. His beautiful tribute, long in the making (he accumulated details for nearly five years), was the result of a total immersion in the work of the Puritan poet and of the history of Colonial America. It has about it, as a result, an authority and a degree of erudition that both attracted and puzzled readers at its first appearance in *Partisan Review* in 1953. (This was the year of the poet's first divorce, caused, at least in part, according to William Martz, by tensions related to the work's slow and difficult composition.) [2] The poem was published without notes and with no introductory apparatus, and as a result the demands it made were very rigorous indeed. It created some interest, but this was limited to the small audience of journal readers.

It was following the publication three years later as a book, with suggestive (though hardly exhaustive) notes, that the poem attracted the attention of major critics and became something of a literary event. *The Times Literary Supplement,* operating under its former policy of ex cathedra anonymity, called it a path-breaking masterpiece. Robert Fitzgerald, at whose home much of the poem was written, called it "the poem of his generation," [3] and Edmund Wilson, the most influential critic in the country, described it as "the most distinguished long poem by an American since *The Waste Land.*" [4] John Holmes, in the *New York Times Book Review,* used the phrase "miniature 'Wasteland,'" and R. W. Flint, in the *New Republic,* called it "a wonderful poem [that] should be read by anyone who thinks that contemporary poets can only work in marble or plaster." [5] Conrad Aiken labelled it a "classic," Robert Lowell "a very big achievement," and Stanley Kunitz "an important poem . . . impressive in its ambition and virtuosity." [6] There were some predictable reservations—John Ciardi, for example, complained that the compressed rhythms create "problems as well as splendors" [7]—but for the most part the critical response was positive to a degree pleasing even to an artist who throughout his life required the most unqualified sort of reinforcement. With the publication of this book he suddenly and spectacularly emerged as a major figure in contemporary letters.

The book itself is extraordinarily handsome—Berryman was clearly fortunate in his publisher. The stanzas, numbered and separated by black lines, are printed one or two to a page on good paper. The print is large and solid, the numerous capital letters, dashes, italics, and ampersands standing out from the bold letters. The stanzas are illustrated by six full-page and three half-page pen and ink drawings by Ben Shahn which, as Louise Bogan wrote, "bring out the lovely and dour side of life in the early Massachusetts Bay Colony in a masterly way." [8] One of the larger illustrations, of a typical Colonial clapboard house backed by black, bare trees, is used on the jacket cover. The drawings, of flowers, trees, citizens, an Indian, are taken from details in the poem, though in a general rather than specific way. Typical Shahn work, they are simple, clear, and primitive (in a sophisticated way), and set up an illuminating contrast with the compressed, highly wrought language. One of the pictures, of a Jack-in-the-Pulpit, was chosen for the cover of the Noonday paperback of the poem; it is all that survives of Shahn in this less elegant, more functional volume in which the stanzas, printed three to a page, lose some of their visual impact.

The poem's stanza is composed of eight highly compressed lines filled with jagged rhythms, puns, repeated words, assonance, allusions, rhetorical climaxes, rhymes, and slant rhymes. The rhythms and the rhyme schemes vary subtly from stanza to stanza, but all the stanzas, or virtually all, share certain characteristics. In all but two (and in these the absence of closure is significant) the first and final lines rhyme, thus giving each small unit, even those eleven without end punctuation, a sense of self-containment. The first and last lines of the final stanza end with the word "loves," the repetition producing a sense of resolution even firmer than that created by rhyme. Each stanza is thus a small push forward, the momentum slowed briefly before the insistent advance begins again.

This overall sense of acceleration and retardation is reinforced by the measure of the individual lines and by frequent punctuation. In each stanza the first two lines, often fairly regular iambic but in any case containing five strong stresses, give way to the shorter third line, made up of three stresses, so that the initial motion is brought to a semi-halt. The momentum then increases gradually in the fourth line, of four stresses, accelerates in the fifth and sixth, which have five stresses each, and is then again balked in the short seventh line, an echo of the third, with three stresses, often in as few as four words. The conclusion then resolves the sense of flow and stasis with a long line, six stresses, that moves slowly and deliberately, resembling nothing so much as an alexandrine, toward the final word, with its small resolution. What Berryman was seeking in this stanza was "something at once flexible and grave, intense and quiet, able to deal with matter both high and low." [9]

This structure precludes a hurried reading. The insistence on intensity and deliberation, the sense of a language that moves irresistibly but slowly rather than with fluid speed, is underscored by the unusually large number of caesurae. There is an average of 12.7 punctuation marks in each stanza, which, in crude terms, comes to something between one and two per line, and though obviously there are lines with none, some with several, the result is incantatory poetry of a high seriousness, of a stately deliberateness that is both majestic and demanding. One important result of this general strategy is to free the verse for more spontaneous movement when such acceleration is called for. Thus the magnificent twentieth stanza, part of a central passage to which everything in the poem is related, a stanza describing the moment of giving birth, when the child "passes the wretched trap whelming," contains only one pause. This exhilarating openness is given particular emphasis by the staccato quality of the stanzas that precede it, dealing with the woman's barrenness, her slow pregnancy, and the strain of her early labor. It is the only place in the poem where the language is permitted to flow, and the only place in which such movement is appropriate.

Why is the work presented in such a deliberate manner? The measured, tentative quality of the language is suited to the drama it records, a dialogue taking place, out of time and out of space, between two poets, one living, the other, summoned from the past, shimmering for an intense duet and then disappearing. Berryman had two mistresses while he was working on this poem. His carnal relationship with "Lise" is celebrated privately in language that, as I have suggested, is often glib, colloquial, racy. This was a love that dared not speak its name, at least publicly.

Anne Bradstreet, more muse than mistress, is the object of intensities more intellectual than physical. Although the poem, not
unlike Marvell's famous argument, is couched as a seduction—
with the added frisson of being an adulterous one, the poet
wooing Anne not only out of history but away from Simon and
her family—the relationship, charming and literary, raises no
questions about moral behavior. The work is a variation on and at
the same time a reversal of the sonnets, the one of celebration of
art, of the power of the imagination to transcend the limitations of
the flesh, the other a celebration, one meant to be private, of a
physical relationship that could never achieve public sanction.
The works are essentially products of the two Berrymans, the
man and the artist; some of the intensities of his "respectable"
seduction of the spirit of Anne Bradstreet derive from the experience, which he was unable to reveal explicitly, of his adulterous
affair with Lise.

The poem falls into five fairly self-contained sections. The first,
stanzas one through four, is an invocation by the poet, or, more
accurately, a conjuring, in which Anne Bradstreet, long dead, is
summoned from her grave. Section two, beginning in the final
line of stanza 4 and ending in stanza 25, is a monologue by Anne,
interrupted only once, when Berryman comments on her appalling didactic verse. The heart of the poem, stanzas 25 through 39,
consists of an eloquent duet in which the poets converse like
lovers in highly charged, often erotic language—Berryman has
referred to the dialogue as "a sort of extended witch-seductress
and demon-lover bit." [10] There is a dramatic shift to a new section in the middle of stanza 39, as Anne succumbs to the strong
pull of the past and Berryman drops out of the poem. This fourth
section closes, with fused imagery of birth and death, in stanza
53. The poem's final four stanzas make up a coda, or peroration,
in which Berryman's voice reappears, bringing several of the
work's images together in a beautifully cadenced conclusion.

The first four stanzas describe a resurrection, the final four a burial, and these related sections, narrated with high seriousness by a deeply moved poet, comprise an elegant frame for the poem. This pairing of parts is repeated in the long second and fourth sections, the halves of Bradstreet's monologue, which are separated by the passionate dialogue of section three. Thus the work as a whole is in the shape of an arch, the line of descent reversing the line of ascent (Berryman, Bradstreet, dialogue, Bradstreet, Berryman), giving the poem an overall form and sense of closure that help account for its aesthetic power. Were the two Bradstreet sections of equal length the sense of classical harmony would be even more pronounced, though it is right that the second monologue, concerned with decay and dissolution, should be shorter in duration than the first one, which creates a sense of the new world settled by the pilgrims.

The exordium opens with the poet, alone in an unspecified place, addressing the spirit of Bradstreet, summoning her across the centuries until she becomes so palpably real to him that his voice, gentle, loving, incantatory, gives way to her own.[11] He sees her in four distinct visions, the final one so vivid that they are joined in a timeless union. He first imagines her in her grave "still" (the word functioning on two levels) awaiting Simon, who outlived her by many years. Then he pictures her in front of a fire reading Sylvester and Quarles, the principle influences on her tedious work, while outside "the New World winters in grand dark." The third vision focuses on her mild eyes as he summons to him her body, now metamorphosed to "maize & air." Finally, he imagines her, young and pockmarked, on the "haggard deck," as the pilgrim boat approaches the American shore. At this point his voice modulates into hers, and she begins her narrative with a description of the journey.

These evocative opening stanzas set the stage for the poem, suggesting the "climate" of the New World, and also introducing images that are played on and resolved later on. The word "still," which ends three of the lines in the first stanza, reappears in the final stanza ("Hover, utter, still, / a sourcing"), the cyclical movement clearly being intentional. A touching line in the second stanza, "foxes down foxholes sigh," is transformed, in stanza 55, to "foxholes hold men," the change suggesting something of the unnatural and violent contemporary scene, transformed from the winter landscape (dangerous in different ways) of the New World winter. And the reference to Simon in the poem's opening line is picked up in stanza 56, "Simon lived on for years." These details and others close the circle of the poem, giving an impression of orderly resolution.

The second section, Anne Bradstreet's first monologue, twenty stanzas in length, begins with her describing the difficult voyage, the drowning of Henry Winthrop, and the dreadful hardships of the first New England summer and winter, with their hunger, fear, storms. She gradually becomes more intimate, touching on such things as her barren state (the first child was not conceived until five years after the marriage), her childhood conversion experience ("I found my heart more carnal and sitting loose from God"), Simon's courtship, her domestic duties, theological disputes. These details all lead to the center of the work, the birth passage to which all other elements are related. This section is introduced by a remarkable image that suggests the distance between her submissive behavior and her actual feelings:

> I revolt from, I am like, these savage foresters
>
> whose passionless dicker in the shade, whose glance
> impassive & scant, belie their murderous cries
> when quarry seems to show.

The cathartic lines end with the completion of labor: "Blossomed Sarah, and I / blossom. Is that thing alive? I hear a famisht howl." The howl relates the passage to the image early in the

monologue of "a fatherless child unkennelled." And the reference
to Sarah varies an earlier Biblical allusion, "and I am Ruth /
away," with its implicit suggestion of an alien country.

There is a falling action after the birth, as Anne Bradstreet
reminisces about more ordinary details, such as those relating to
theological disputes and attitudes toward death. Stanza 24 introduces Anne Hutchinson, whom Berryman turns into one of
Anne Bradstreet's dearest friends, though there is no historical
evidence to support this supposed relationship. (The poet takes a
good many liberties with history.) Anne Hutchinson was exiled to
Rhode Island in 1638 (she is one of the founders of the state)
because of her unorthodox religious views; she got into the technical doctrinal debate over the issue of grace versus works, and
was denounced (as much for sedition as heresy) when she admit-
ted to having experienced personal revelation. A rebel against ac-
ceptable modes of conduct, not just for women but for the citi-
zenry generally, she is one of the most courageous and influential
women in American history. Anne Bradstreet's address to her
moves the poem from the general realm to the personal, and provides an opportunity for Berryman, who has been silent and attentive, to approach her in an intimate manner; he has been
awaiting his chance, and the emotional assertion of loss provides
an opening:

> Bitter sister, victim! I miss you.
> —I miss you, Anne,
> day or night weak as a child,
> tender & empty, doomed, quick to no tryst.
> —I hear you. Be kind, you who leaguer
> my image in the mist.
> —Be kind you, to one unchained eager far & wild
>
> and if, O my love, my heart is breaking, please
> neglect my cries and I will spare you. Deep
> in Time's grave, Love's, you lie still.

Lie still.—Now? That happy shape
my forehead had under my most long, rare,
ravendark, hidden, soft bodiless hair
you award me still.
You must not love me, but   I do not bid you cease.

The pause in the final line is crucial, suggesting the tension between the woman's sense of propriety and restraint and her willingness to be moved by this affectionate stranger who leaguers
(besieges) her image in the mist. The love duet, sustaining the intensity of these opening exchanges, continues for fourteen stanzas, ending in number 39 with a very broad transition in the
phrase "Jane is so slipshod," which reunites Anne with her past
(the pull being too powerful for her would-be lover to overcome),
and at this point Berryman drops out of the poem until his valedictory coda.

During the dialogue the speakers are always clearly distinguished, each change of voice indicated (rather the way indenta-
tion shows a new speaker in prose dialogue) by a dash, usually at
the beginning of a line, though sometimes within. (I found in the
classroom that having two students read the "roles" dispels immediately any confusion about who says what.) Berryman speaks
eleven times, Anne nine. When the dialogue is at its most intense the responses come quickly, in the manner of stichomythia.
At other times, each speaker develops ideas in short arias which
then evoke responses, of varying length, from the listener.

Considering that this is a conversation between "lovers" it is in
some respects very strange indeed. Anne is torn between her
desire to be loved, to be regarded as a woman, and her feeling,
the inevitable result of her heritage, that her response is
"wicked." Thus her talk shifts from the breathlessly erotic to
images of retching, fainting, "a manic slouch," the fruits of her
revolt. When these memories recede her language once again
becomes seductive:

> And out of this I lull. It lessens. Kiss me.
> That once. As sings out up in sparkling dark
> a trail of a star & dies,
> while the breath flutters, sounding, mark,
> so shorn ought such caresses to us be
> who, deserving nothing, flush and flee
> the darkness of that light,
> a lurching frozen from a warm dream. Talk to me.

This leads into one of Berryman's most evocative passages, "—It is Spring's New England," in turn followed by a series of short exchanges that moves into the crucial stanza 33, in which the poet, "drowning in this past" and losing sight of his new "mistress," likens himself to a disoriented diver who offers passing fish his equipment. This is followed by one of the more striking passages, that in which the focus shifts from the "wickedness" of the mistress to that of her lover. In confessional lines that anticipate the dream songs, the poet speaks of trundling bodies over fire: "I wonder if *I* killed him." Anne assures him that he is "good," but he nevertheless launches into a bitter and hopeless lament in which he sounds more like Henry than like the affectionate poet who conjures his mistress out of maize & air—it is clear that he is seeking not only a lover but a listener as well:

> . . . Many is entirely alone
> may be. I am a man of griefs & fits
> trying to be my friend. And the brown smock splits,
> down the pale flesh a gash
> broadens and Time holds up your heart against my eyes.

This bizarre image evokes from Anne, wavering between hostility toward God and surrender to His will, three stanzas filled with nightmare images of Nazi tortures, of pestles smashing "small women swarming towards the mortar's rim in vain," "cruel spread Wings," and horrors that "warp" down stormy air. In stanza 39 the struggle is resolved:

. . . Evil dissolves, & love, like foam;
that love. Prattle of children powers me home,
my heart claps like the swan's
under a frenzy of *who* love me & who shine.

At this point Berryman temporarily disappears from the poem, the next fourteen stanzas being Anne's monologue, this time more a soliloquy than the first long speech, which is addressed to her fellow poet.

The passage, filled with domestic details, focuses largely on small events in the lives of her children (Mercy, young Simon, and Samuel) as they confront the mysteries of life and ask troubling questions about death. There is in these stanzas an appealing sense of maternal tranquility (it is her children and not her "proportioned, spiritless poems" that engage her attention) even though the themes of disease and death loom large in many lines, always threatening to crowd the serenity off the page. There is a description of her father's death, of "vomitings, trots, rashes," of piles, and of baby John breaking out, but these details are treated with a kind of tough-minded resignation that belies self-pity or despair. Anne's faith, even though it is at times sorely tried, sustains her through the crises involving sickness and death.

Beginning with the phrase "Iller I, oftener," in stanza 46, the focus shifts to her own physical deterioration, and this subject dominates the last seven stanzas of the section, those just preceding the coda, which is actually a funeral oration. She describes her "sore breath," her "body a-drain," and moments of fever ("I sniff a fire burning without outlet, / consuming acrid its own smoke. It's me"), delirium, incontinence, pain ("my wreckt chest hurts when Simon pales"). Stanza 51 eloquently describes the nature of her heart disease (the "pacemaker," Berryman tells us in a note, is her heart itself) and records the period of quiet that precedes the agony of her dying:

> My window gives on the graves, in our great new house
> (how many burned?) upstairs, among the elms.
> I lie, & endure, & wonder.
> A haze slips sometimes over my dreams
> and holiness on horses' bells shall stand.
> Wandering pacemaker, unsteadying friend,
> in a redskin calm I wait:
> beat when you will our end. Sinkings & droopings drowse.

This "redskin calm" is lost in the powerful stanza, composed of short, lucid phrases, in which she drifts toward death. Since birth and death are central themes in the poem it is formally appropriate and aesthetically satisfying to find in this quiet stanza an image that evokes the euphoric birth sequence:

> . . . I'll—I'll—
> I am closed & coming. Somewhere! I defile
> wide as a cloud, in a cloud,
> unfit, desirous, glad—even the singings veil—

At this moment her voice stops, she retreats back to the grave from which she has been summoned, and the poet speaks his brief and loving eulogy: "You are not ready? You are ready. Pass, / as shadow gathers shadow in the welling night."

The four stanzas of the coda contain some of the most haunting language in the poem. The first, spoken as if at graveside ("We commit our sister down"), introduces fireflies, shadow, and a lover's candle, and these lovely images reappear in the final stanza, giving the coda the same sort of self-contained cyclical movement that characterizes the work as a whole. The second stanza, in which the tone shifts dramatically, is very odd, gaining its effects from a cluster of words that relate to intoxication: stagger, draughts, pass out, reel, blind, chilling. This passage leads into the lines describing the horrors of the poet's private and public worlds:

> . . . Already with the wounded flying
> dark air fills, I am a closet of secrets dying,
> races murder, foxholes hold men,
> reactor piles wage slow upon the wet brain rime.

The final two stanzas, shifting the focus back to the "old world," and to Anne, who draws off "a benevolent phantom," repeat words and phrases ("Simon lived on," "still") from the poem's opening, and end with an exordium that is not so much an evocation as a resolution, an expression of reconciliation: "Hover, utter, still, / a sourcing   whom my lost candle like the firefly loves."

How exactly was Anne Bradstreet "a sourcing" for Berryman, and why did he choose to pay homage to her? In an interview printed in the *Minnesota Daily* (a student newspaper) in 1956, he said he had no particular reason for selecting her "except that she was the first poet of this country and that her great effort to create, to exercise her intellect is to be greatly admired. She lived in a society which frowned on a woman's interest going beyond the home, where harsh circumstances made survival of prime importance." [12] On another occasion he said he did not choose her, but that she chose him, and that he was concerned with her, "almost from the beginning, as a woman, not much as a poetess." [13] He is clearly more interested in her rebellion than in her extraordinarily dull work; she manifested in her life the sort of tough-minded independence that she never achieved in her poetry. He has shown her in a series of defiant moments, rebelling against youthful virtue, the new environment, an arranged marriage, her barrenness, her confinement to household duties, a life of illness and loss, and against God's will. The submission, or capitulation, that follows each of these brave moments establishes one of the basic rhythms of the poem, that is, a sequence of alternating assertions and defeats. [14]

Berryman's knowledge of Anne Bradstreet's rebellion derives largely from a biography by Helen Campbell and from study of the Winthrop papers, including narratives and town histories. He also made a thorough analysis of her "bald abstract didactic rime," working into his poem lines and details from her work. In stanza 8, for example, he uses a passage that appears in Bradstreet's Meditation 53, taken from scripture:

> I know whom I have trusted, & whom I have believed,
> and that he is able to
> keep   that I have committed to his charge.

Bradstreet uses "His" but otherwise the passage is quoted verbatim; it is remarkable how well it fits into the Berryman stanza. The final line of stanza 13 and the first line of 14 are also direct quotations: "I found my heart more carnal and sitting loose from God, / vanity & the follies of youth took hold of me." The phrase "Motes that hop in sunlight slow" (in stanza 9) is a variation of a Bradstreet line, "Every mote in sunlight hops," and other of Berryman's homely domestic images also derive from her work.[15]

What is most impressive is the way he manages to create, out of shards, borrowed images, Hopkinsesque rhythms, and his own imagination, a language that so effectively evokes the atmosphere—social, religious, political—of her era. As Hyatt Waggoner says, the best way to approach Anne Bradstreet is to begin with Berryman's poem: "This vivid and moving tribute by a contemporary poet to a poetic ancestor brings the wife and mother alive as her own verse seldom does even in the best known of her few personal poems like 'To My Dear and Loving Husband.' In Berryman's poem we get the existential life that is generally buried under the theology and borrowed imagery of Mrs. Bradstreet's own verse writing."[16] It would not have been appropriate for the poet to pay his homage by imitating his subject's work, aware as he was of her derivative blandness. He chose, instead, to discover the energy and passion that, realized in Anne Bradstreet's life, are only potential in her work. He created a voice that, had she been born under different stars, might well have been her own.

CHAPTER 4

The Lonely Laments of Henry Pussycat

I fink it's bads all over

I

In a moving foreword to *Recovery*, Berryman's posthumous novel, Saul Bellow says that what his friend needed for his art "had been supplied by his own person, by his mind, his wit. He drew it out of his vital organs, out of his very skin. At last there was no more." [1] Surely no work was ever more thoroughly drawn from a writer's physical self than *The Dream Songs*. The poet, with his awful conscience, virtually flays himself. "We are using our own skins for wallpaper and we cannot win," he says in Song 53, quoting Gottfried Benn but clearly relating the image to himself. His verse is referred to as "Henry's pelt put on sundry walls" and as "all my blood in pawn." "I write with my stomach," he announces, and quotes Renoir, "I paint with my penis." Skin, pelt, blood, stomach, penis, and the ever present bones—the songs are built with pieces of the poet. At last there was no more. [2]

There are 385 dream songs in the published collection, created by and out of the poet. They document, in the manner of a journal or diary, his chaotic life in progress, one full of self-pity, rage, laughter, resentment, and love. In beginning this huge work Berryman had no more idea where it would ultimately go, what it would contain, than has Henry, his speaker, of where his muddled life will go, or what it will contain. The book progresses, as Henry tells us in number 293, not in the manner of cliffhangers or old serials, "but according to his nature." As in the nature of anyone who takes very large risks, however, there is a good deal of cliffhanging involved, both for reader and for poet, much of the suspense residing in the question of whether Henry House, huffing and puffing, will manage to blow himself down. The tension is resolved when the "huffy" speaker of the opening poem, "wicked & away," and unwilling to come out and talk, becomes, by the final poem, a mellower Henry who, holding his heavy daughter, realizes that his house is "well made."

It is the prerogative of any maker to let his materials, as he goes along, discover their own form, one that may well reflect his own nature. The design of the songs, unlike that for the nearly symmetrical tribute to Anne Bradstreet, was imposed *ex post facto*. It quite clearly is not the product of a detailed blueprint. William Meredith, who was with the poet at Bread Loaf during the summer of 1962, and who day by day heard new songs recited (sometimes at 4 A.M.), says that not until the end of the summer did Berryman attempt to find the structure of what had been up to then an improvisational work.[3] The poems emerged, were uttered, bloomed, almost spontaneously over a period of many years. Sitting all night in his green chair, puffing on Tareytons and drinking either bourbon or coffee, Berryman brought forth songs the way a tree produces leaves, in the process scattering pages, and ashes, all over the rug. Only much later did he take on the tasks of selection, revision, and rejection, finally gathering the "parts" into the order that makes up the completed sequence. There were many more songs written than are found in the book; several, some very fine, have been published during the last two years in *The New Yorker, The Times Literary Supplement, Atlantic* and *American Poetry Review,* and others will emerge over the years. What interests me here are those that Berryman chose to include in his massive work, and the order in which he placed them.

The 77 *Dream Songs,* published in 1964, were written before nearly all of the songs that appeared four years later in *His Toy, His Dream, His Rest;* some of the later work, in fact, comments on responses to the earlier book. The poems, however, are not for the most part placed in the order in which they were composed, nor are they organized around any clearly delimited period of time, such as a year in Berryman's life. Section seven ends in fall, which, given Henry's age and mood, is where it should end (it is the blight man was born for), but the book begins in medias res, and although we know that Berryman wrote songs for eleven years we do not know how much "internal" time elapses between the first section and the last, nor is the question either very important or very interesting.

The individual sections (which I will also refer to as "books" and as "parts"), made up of 26, 25, 26, 14, 54, 132, and 106 songs, are terminated for reasons of aesthetics and rhythm. Each suggests in microcosm the overall pattern of the work as a whole, moving from a prying open to a resolution, from imagery of arrival and spring to that of departure and autumn. Each ends with a sense of summing up, a moment of stasis, and it is this stasis, or suspension of process, that the beginning of each new section disrupts in images of renewal. To be specific, section one, which begins with images of the sea (invariably associated with Berryman's parents), of an oyster (or coffin, or patient) "pried open," and of a bird in a sycamore, closes twenty-five poems later with a song that reintroduces the singing bird motif ("The glories of the world struck me, made me aria, once") and that then suggests, symbolically, an end of singing: "—I had a most marvellous   piece of luck. I died." If the work is to continue there clearly must be some sort of resurrection or rebirth. The opening poem of the second section satisfies this necessity, bringing the work back to life with the lush line, "The greens of the Ganges delta foliate." "Green" appears in each of the three stanzas, accounting for the poem's vitality. To leave no doubt, moreover, about whether the sequence has been resurrected, the song ends "while good Spring / returns with a dance and a sigh." The new section, despite its promising beginning, is filled with images of loss and death, and by its final poem the dance of Spring has given way to "dwarfs' dead times" and to seas that, far from being fructuous and life-giving, are "remorseless." The song's last stanza brings the reader up short with a comic, Beckett-like catechism that seems to leave little possibility for continuation:

> —Are you radioactive, pal? —Pal, radioactive.
> —Has you the night sweats & the day sweats, pal?
> —Pal, I do.
> —Did your gal leave you? —What do *you* think, pal?
> —Is that thing on the front of your head what it
> > seems to be, pal?
> —Yes, pal.

The third section commences with Henry awakening, yet another resurrection of sorts, and though its general mood is one of lamentation, the opening song closes with references to the "thing" (Henry's loss) counterpoised against "spring mist, warm rain." Henry, and his songs, are up and about again. The final poem of 77 *Dream Songs* (and thus of section three), though set "in a world of Fall," actually sounds like an opening song, and with good reason, since too strong a sense of closure at this point would block the poet's (and Henry's) options. And so Berryman indicates, in assertive images, that though this book is finished there is more to come: "his head full / & his heart full, he's making ready to move on." No longer huffy, Henry is now "seedy" (ill-kempt, but also full of life), stripped down and impenitent. He is barely getting started, a fact borne out by the publication, four years later, of *His Toy, His Dream, His Rest.*

Section four, the "Op. Posth." poems that introduce the new volume, continues this reversal of the ascent-descent scheme, its opening song, number 78, dealing not with renewal and spring but with physical and mental diminution, with castration and decay: "Henry's parts were fleeing." Song 91, the last of these remarkable messages from the grave, opens with Henry being dug up (pried open once more for all the world to see), exposed again to the awful world of taxes, bills, and insurance. A stunning final stanza brings the book to a conclusion that is simultaneously funny and unnerving:

> A fortnight later, sense a single man
> upon the trampled scene at 2 a.m.
> insomnia-plagued, with a shovel
> digging like mad, Lazarus with a plan
> to get his own back, a plan, a stratagem
> no newsman will unravel.

This short section of fourteen songs (most of which were published originally in *The Times Literary Supplement*) serves as a link between the first three parts and the final three. Book five, following the picture of reverse-Lazarus, opens with number 92, "Room 231: the forth week." It documents a symbolic faring forth or resurrection—Henry, suffocating in his hospital room, yearning for oblivion, and still as his cadaver, nevertheless "waking to march." A new series is thus initiated. The book ends fifty-three songs later with a suicide. It is not Henry who seeks the grave this time, however, but his father ("I touch now his despair"), who one summer dawn, unable to bear life an instant longer, "rose with his gun and went outdoors by my window / and did what was needed," leaving his despairing son to live on miserably. The song ends, like section three, with the assurance of more to come, but the detailed images of the successful suicide create a strong sense of finality. The placement of these opening and closing songs is always anything but arbitrary.

As if in conscious response to his own preoccupation with the death of his father and of others, and with his own life-in-death state, Henry insists, at the beginning of book six, that he is not in hell, that he is "lively," and that "I have not done." "Down with them all!" he says about his dead friends, and this expression of seemingly heartless dismissal is the most notable example in the poem (there are others) of his attempt to resist the nearly overpowering attractions of the tomb. That this attempt to escape the tyranny of the dead is extremely short-lived is demonstrated by a block of twelve poems that follows, an anguished series of eulogies addressed to his friend Delmore Schwartz: "I can't get him out of my mind, out of my mind."

The sixth book comes to a conclusion with three "Farewell" poems, and again the source of the emotion is the loss of friends. This time, however, it is not death but departure that causes the separation: some "pals" and their wives are going to California to teach, and Henry, grinning at "green friends" in Dublin, wishes them well, hoping they will be spared the academic infighting that has resulted in "one decade's war" at his university. The last farewell ends with an image of a queen bee swarming to the west, leaving Henry behind. The closing lines are reminiscent of the end of the first song, though by now the sea, the source of life, is also associated with John Smith's death, and thus suggests as well the attractions of oblivion: "Pardon my sore toast, nominal & blunt / & let's get on toward the sea." (It is not possible to read any of Berryman's ocean and river songs without experiencing a sense of foreboding.)

Book seven opens with a faring forth that is, for once, literal. Aboard a liner bound for Europe, "Leaving behind the country of the dead," Henry sets his face due East. (Since the sequence, as I have suggested, moves intuitively rather than logically or even chronologically, it need not concern us that Berryman has already placed Henry in Dublin at the very end of book six.) The voyage is in part a pilgrimage to Yeats (the late poetry is one of five books Henry takes abroad) and thus there is a nice irony in the fact that Yeats himself "voyaged" from Ireland because it is "no country for old men," leaving behind the young in one another's arms in his quest for a world of unaging intellect. For his part, Henry leaves the country of the dead, "where he must then return & die himself," seeking a new world where he will craft better, answer letters, and spend a whole year "tense with love." The exuberance of this opening song, with its resolutions and sense of hope, is touching since by now the reader knows that the good intentions, like all of Henry's promises, are destined to be casualties of his rage for disorder.

The book ends, in the fall, with references to Henry's house and to the sea (bringing the work full cycle), and with the beautifully resonant final words, "my heavy daughter." While Pound's *Cantos* or Williams' *Paterson* could have continued almost indefinitely, it is not possible to imagine a reopening of the *Songs* after number 385, so absolute is the sense of closure. The last farewell is set up by several songs that precede it, all of which document a gradual retardation and give a sense of summing up. Number 381, for example, which opens with the image of "a house," contains these ominously understated lines: "I am frightened by the waves upon the shore, / & seldom steal there, wetter / with the wild rain but safe, & back to the cave." (The sea and shelter, like fear and love, are always pictured as polar opposites in Henry's mind.) In the next poem he imagines his own funeral. Number 383 refers to "the end of the labour," and introduces his daughter. In the penultimate poem, in a grotesque scene similar to that revealing Lazarus digging madly in the earth (and reminiscent of Sylvia Plath's "Daddy"), we find Henry, enraged, spitting at his father's flowerless grave, imagining himself tearing open the casket and crashing an ax into the remains, thus playing his "final card." His fury purged by this cathartic action, he moves to the gentle autumnal melancholy of the final poem, playing as yet one more card not a club but a heart:

> My daughter's heavier. Light leaves are flying.
> Everywhere in enormous numbers turkeys will be dying
> and other birds, all their wings.
> They never greatly flew. Did they wish to?
> I should know. Off away somewhere once I knew
> such things.

It is Henry we grieve for.

II

Who is this man of sorrows and fears, this armchair explorer whose salutations and farewells establish the structure of the seven books? Berryman named him Henry, he says in a *Paris Review* interview, not in deference to Henry James, or Lieutenant Henry, or Henry Fleming, but because his second wife, Ann, nicknamed him Henry. (He countered with "Mabel"; they agreed that these were the most awful names anyone could be called. An early dream song about Henry and Mabel is not included in the final selection.) Henry's full name is Henry House,[4] but he has other monikers as well. He is Henry Cat, Pussycat (Jarrell's name for Berryman), Henry of Donnybrook, Sir Henry, Senator Cat, Henry Hankovitch, and once, like a signature worked into a painting, he is John. Henry is also Mr. Bones, Sir Bones, Dr. Bones, Brother Bones, and Galahad. The character who uses these sobriquets is an inquisitive friend who appears intermittently, mostly in the first three sections (he all but disappears in the later books), jumping up and down like an end man in a minstrel show, and offering words of counsel or reproof. Either black or in blackface, he speaks a thick stage-Negro dialect. He represents a kind of Job's comforter, saying, for the most part, altogether reasonable and not always supportive things that Henry, irrepressibly irrational and vulnerable, does not especially want to hear. Their dialogue is between mind and body, superego and id, realist and dreamer. Even the name (Mr. Bones) given him by his sober sidekick is a constant reminder of Henry's erotic excesses as well as, more importantly, his mortality. With such friends Sir Henry has little need of foes.

He also has friends who *are* supportive, however, some of whom he constantly addresses as "Pal," and these are such nonfictional individuals as William (Meredith), Adrienne (Rich), Saul (Bellow), Dwight (McDonald), Boyd and Maris (Thomes). In addition there are a distressingly large number of friends and literary heroes who have been taken away by his archenemy, God, and many of the lonely laments of Senator Cat are eulogies for intimates, notably Delmore Schwartz, Randall Jarrell, Richard Blackmur, and for others less close such as Roethke, Hemingway, Williams, Frost, and Plath. Dylan Thomas, surprisingly, is mentioned only twice, in passing.

Like Chekhov's Masha, Henry is also in mourning for his own disorderly life, and poem by harried poem we discover why. He has suffered an "irreversible loss," we learn in the note to *His Toy, His Dream, His Rest,* and though we never find out exactly what this is, the evidence suggests that it is related to his father's suicide, the loss that "wiped out" his childhood and filled his adult life with dread and rage. Henry himself is suicidal, often so anxious and depressed that he can barely make it through the night. (Like Samuel Beckett, he can deal with this depression

only by probing deep into its sources.) He is architect of his own
dishonor, and his life is a shambles. His lusts, like those of a tom-
cat, are unappeasable, and his infidelities have contributed to the
destruction of two marriages. He also has a classic alcoholic personality, drinking far too much and behaving terribly when
drunk; all attempts to stay "off the sauce" are doomed. He is accident prone, spending a lot of time in hospitals getting broken
limbs mended. People try to put things over on him. He is "at
odds wif de world & its god," is bored, and is ravaged by guilt.
He is so constituted that he can never efface any painful sensation
from his memory, try as he will. He can't sleep. He has day
sweats and night sweats, and constantly experiences fear and
panic. He is Lazarus with a plan to get his own back, but himself
is hell, and which way he flies, or digs, is hell. The adjectives that
describe him help tell the tale—he is transient Henry, horrible
Henry ("the brain from hell"), wilful Henry, criminal Henry,
troubled and gone Henry, monstrous bug, abominable & impenetrable Henry, stricken Henry, ridiculous Henry.

Confronted with such loathing and suicidal despair, note-
worthy even in a generation of depressives, it is possible to
overlook the somewhat gentler sides of things. If one of Berryman's sources is Rilke, the great poet of death, he was also
deeply affected by "Song of Myself," that great poem of life.
Henry is a complex sensibility who at odd moments even sees
himself as gentle, friendly, savage & thoughtful, happy & idle,
imperishable. He is Rabbi Henry, and once pictures himself as
"the steadiest man in the block." Dedicated to tasting all the
secret bits of life, he experiences on rare occasions "moments of
supreme joy." His highs, like his lows, are extreme, not surprising in a performer addicted to self-dramatization, and, like all
theatrical personalities, given to bursts of melodrama, hyperbole,
and uninhibited self-revelation. He is, moreover, addicted to au-
totherapy, and the songs represent, as much as anything else, at-

tempts to get his dreams, memories, and fears out in the open as a means of coming to grips with them, of escaping their tyranny. (I say Henry and mean Berryman. I think that anyone who reads the songs carefully will reject the assertion that they are about an imaginary character—some details, of course, are invented, but the sequence adheres closely to the facts of the poet's life and mind.) The vitality, grave comedy, and outright buffoonery of many of the songs vitiate against an uncritical acceptance of the nightmares they contain. Like those Romantic odes on dejection that by their existence give a lie to the assertion that the sufferer is rendered incapable of creation, many of these songs, in their wit and high spirits, ward off the horror that is their source. It is, however, because the nightmares are recounted, the terrors revealed, the guilt expressed, that Henry, patient and analyst, confessor and priest, is able to go on dreaming and muddling through. He is "obliged to perform in complete darkness / operations of great delicacy." The operations are on himself, and somehow, God knows how, he manages to endure. He is blessed, at the very least, with nine lives.

The reader, willing or not, becomes a participant in this therapeutic process, sitting as silent auditor and monitoring the material in an effort to discover and understand its mysteries and patterns. He (or she) is likely to be alternately (and sometimes simultaneously) edified, amused, baffled, moved, bored, and spellbound. He is also likely to experience those spasms of impatience that are the lot of anyone, be he analyst, ombudsman, bartender, parent, or priest, who is sentenced to long terms of conscientious listening. An attentive reader is also almost certain, particularly if he is a middle-aged, heterosexual academic whose life is not without a certain amount of chaos, to experience a powerful sense of identification with the poet. And if he is especially sensitive, capable of unusual empathy, he may well get under Henry's skin (pelt), may discover what it feels like to *be* Henry, how it feels, literally, to want to jump out of one's skin. It is because such a reader, secure in the quiet of his home, can get outside Henry by an act of spiritual migration (rather than by leaping from a bridge) that this dangerous book is ultimately liberating and even protective. Our lives are all potentially disastrous, and artists like Berryman and Lowell who live perilously close to the abyss make it possible for us to journey over threatening terrain, to experience its terror, and to return intact. Literature does not tell us anything; it permits us to participate in a life, to share an angle of vision, and often to make some crucial personal discoveries. In courting certain kinds of disaster, Henry spares us the necessity of doing so for ourselves, overpowering as the attractions sometimes are.

This idea of salvation through syntax, of having a proxy in purgatory, presupposes that the life experienced at one remove is sufficiently intelligible to invite the sort of identification I have described. On one occasion Henry refers to himself as impenetrable, and on another says "these poems are not meant to be understood you understand." A charge frequently levelled at Berryman is that many of his songs are indeed impenetrable, so that even the most rigorous analysis fails to yield up their secrets. Readers have dismissed the book after encountering passages that make little or no sense. But to return to the image of reader as auditor, it is absolutely necessary to listen carefully, openly, and imaginatively, to listen again, and then to begin to listen. A poem is not a puzzle to be solved, and in any case no amount of footnoting or explication will communicate the power of an intricate song if one is not attentive, first of all, to its sound and shape.[5] There are indeed many passages in Berryman (as there are in Pound and Joyce) that remain baffling, and perhaps impenetrable, even after numerous readings, but if one is responsive to the general spirit of Henry's language and if one listens attentively to the music these should not finally undermine significantly the delight to be derived from the work.

The invocation of Pound is apposite since *The Dream Songs*, in spite of crucial differences in intention and poetic strategy, resembles the *Cantos* more than any other modern sequence, with the possible exception of Lowell's *Notebooks*. The differences are, of course, significant. The *Cantos* contains a history of the world, and the purposes of the work are largely political and didactic. Pound was evangelically committed to rescuing a decadent civilization, largely by bringing about the reform of what he regarded to be a corrupt economic system that perverts virtue and good craftsmanship. His massive epic takes in all times, all cultures, and all lands. Berryman, by contrast, journeys not through eras and across continents but over the blighted terrain of his own personal history. Only rarely political, he clearly has no illusions of rescuing the world, though, like Auden and Yeats, he was dedicated to the preservation of tradition, literary and otherwise. His interest is mainly in rescuing himself from himself. If his songs give a stunningly accurate picture of certain universal aspects of contemporary sensibility, and if they manage to "terrify and comfort," these are important secondary consequences, but not the poet's principal intentions.

The dissimilarities in the two works derive from differences in the writers, and the similarities are literary rather than political. Each is a poem in progress, composed over a long period of time, that develops in concert with the life-in-progress of a protean poet. Each introduces an enormous cast of characters, largely historical in Pound's case, personal and literary in Berryman's. Each is thickly allusive, and each constantly alludes to itself, building up an elaborate network of cross references, repeated images, recurring motifs, and thematic variations. In each the overall effect is cumulative, lines and passages acquiring meaning by what precedes and follows, so that while many individual sections are self-contained (Song 29 or Canto 45, for example) they cannot be understood fully outside the context of the whole work.

Each work, moreover, representing as it does the growth of its maker's mind, is a recreation of that mind—of everything the poet has done, seen, heard, felt, read. It is here that a reader, however sympathetic, is likely to lose his bearings—obviously there is much in the poet's storehouse of recollection that not only has no relation to his own memories or knowledge, but that he has no way of tracking down and mastering. Berryman, like Pound an omniverous reader, was a scholar "who swoops, who browses," a rigorous intellectual in love all his life with erudition. He spent hundreds of hours (and dollars) on books of all sorts, filling his mind up to that moment when, as he says in number 148, "the data (he decided) were abundantly his." We have Bellow's testimony about the "elegant editions of Nashe and Marlowe and Beaumont and Fletcher which John was forever importing from Blackwell's," and of "scorched theology books from a fire sale" that lined the poet's office wall.[6] He was, Richard Kelly tells us, an "avid library user." [7] His special interests were theology, psychology, and religious thought, and to understand several of the poems a reader must be willing to track down some fairly esoteric references—Berryman was a great looter of details, an unembarrassed quarrier. One can accept "Valerie Trueblood," or "the Bhuvaneshwar Dog," or "Addison" pretty much on faith, recognizing that these are real people (or canines) who compose part of what Erving Goffman calls one's "with," and about whom we are almost certain to know only what we are told. We can, however, with a bit of effort, find out something about Gottwald & Co., Hashknife Hartley, Chen Lung, Baal Shem Tov, St. Simeon the Lesser Theologian, Mendel-Wurm, and Abba Pimen (to give a few examples from the first three sections), if we want to understand better the poems in which they appear. Eventually someone will annotate the *Songs,* and we will be able to approach Berryman the way we now can Eliot, whose every syllable, not excluding "Twit twit twit / Jug jug jug jug jug" has been explicated. Meanwhile we must draw on our own resources, compare notes, and use the library.

There are some allusions in the *Songs*, of course, that no amount of conventional research will unlock, which is to be expected in so personal and eccentric a book. In number 3, for example, the phrase "Thick chests quit" derives its point from an article Berryman had recently read in *Life* about the coronary risks of mesomorphs.[8] In number 19 Henry smiles into his mirror, "A murderer's (at Stillwater)," and since Henry constantly identifies with criminals (Speck, Whitman, Loeb, Bogart in *High Sierra*, "Henry got away with murder") the reference requires no gloss. It takes on an added dimension, though, if we know that bachelor Berryman once rented an apartment that had previously been inhabited by a young man who killed his wife, and who was sentenced to Stillwater.[9] In this same poem Henry says "a plink to that desolate fellow." The curious word is a Berryman mannerism—he sometimes responded to a question with "plink." (His alter ego in *Recovery*, Jasper Stone, also uses the word.)

In number 45, "some wired his head / to read a wrong opinion, 'Epileptic' " alludes to a medical diagnosis Berryman received while teaching at Wayne in Detroit in 1940.[10] Number 49 is titled "Blind," which, playing on the idea of being "blind drunk," also continues the theme of sightlessness that runs through the first three sections. The song's final word, "Braille," though requiring no gloss, takes on witty connotations if we know that it represents a telescoping of the name of one of the poet's favorite bars, The Brass Rail. The song in which Henry's mother is idealized, number 100, is set in a "frantic hot / night of the eighth of July" which, it happens, is her birthday. In number 213 we find "the Mayor's wife" sinking "into grateful sleep" by his good side. Again, the lines require no gloss, but it helps to know that the former Mayor of Minneapolis and his wife, Arthur and Fran Naftalin, were among Berryman's closest friends.

There are other private allusions as well. When compared to the personal details in the *Cantos*, however, the references Berryman permits Henry are few and unobtrusive. There may, of course, be many undiscovered references worked into the poem, undiscovered precisely because they are so personal, but it is likely that new information will simply add intensities or levels of meaning to lines (like "Braille") that function effectively without it. Most of the details in the work, however, relate either to information that is given in the poetry itself or to material in the public, as opposed to private, domain. Some songs can be interpreted in isolation, and most of the others in the light of details, tonalities, and images presented in other songs. This is all part of the elaborate network of cross-referencing that makes the parts of the work, loosely organized as they often are, contribute to the whole.

Let me give a few examples, some obvious, others a bit less so, of Berryman's organizational strategies. Song 5 begins with the following stanza, in dialect:

> Henry sats in de bar & was odd,
> off in the glass from the glass,
> at odds wif de world & its god,
> his wife is a complete nothing,
> St Stephen
> getting even.

As in many of the poems the peculiar language, which adds a comic tone to the whisky broodings, presents no obstacles to a reader's comprehension. Henry, sitting at a bar (perhaps The Brass Rail), is reflected in a mirror, which is some distance from his glass of bourbon. He likens himself to St. Stephen, the first Christian martyr, who was stoned to death, and sees himself as "getting even" for his own martyrdom by being at odds with God, and by "getting stoned" in the bar. The "getting even" is played against "was odd," and "at odds," producing a play on "odds and evens." The cruel references to his wife is softened if we notice Henry's habitual baby-talk, as in number 114 ("Henry is weft on his own") and translate "wife" to "life," so that the bitter comment is also self-directed. (It is curious that he also uses "wif," which makes a play with "wife," but not "nuffing." It is never possible to predict exactly where Henry's verbal inventions will take him.)

The sense of self-loathing evident in this stanza is even more powerfully documented in the brilliant 29th song, which begins "There sat down, once, a thing on Henry's heart," this unspecified *thing*, depression, loss, guilt (or perhaps a combination of these) being the major source of Henry's despair. The final stanza is especially revealing.

> But never did Henry, as he thought he did,
> end anyone and hacks her body up
> and hide the pieces, where they may be found.
> He knows; he went over everyone, & nobody's missing.
> Often he reckons, in the dawn, them up.
> Nobody is ever missing.

One of the central themes that joins Plath, Lowell, Roethke, Sexton, Berryman, and other extremist writers (including the Arthur Miller of *After the Fall*) is the sense of guilt that pervades their work, guilt based on the fear that one is somehow personally responsible for the destruction of others and at times, as Karl Malkoff suggests, for a holocaust—that one is a victim, and, ultimately, one's own victim.[11] The lines above describe the morning horrors of an alcoholic who has no memory at all of what he may have done during a blacked-out period the night before, and who automatically fears the worst. Though nobody is ever missing, Henry knows that he is capable of "ending" someone and hacking her up (a recurring misogynous fantasy in Berryman's work), and this helps account for his identification with Speck, who murdered several nurses in Chicago, with the insane Texas sniper Whitman (whose father taught him "respect for guns but not for people"), and with Loeb, who gave himself wholly to crime. One is inevitably reminded of *Life Studies,* in which Robert Lowell expresses a terrible sense of kinship with Czar Lepke of Murder Incorporated. Henry's dawn terrors help explain what his friend has in mind, in number 50, when he pronounces on the dreadfulness of this black art:

> —Mr Bones, your troubles give me vertigo,
> & backache. Somehow, when I make your scene,
> I cave to feel as if
>
> de roses of dawns & pearls of dusks, made up
> by some ol' writer-man, got right forgot
> & the greennesses of ours.

He makes a similar comment at the end of the thirteenth song: "as I look on the saffron sky, / you strikes me as ornery."

Song 66, technically reminiscent of Cummings, adds another dimension to the theme of identification and self-reproach, and gains meaning from the work that precedes it as well as from what follows:

> 'All virtues enter into this world:')
> A Buddhist, doused in the street, serenely burned.
> The Secretary of State for War,
> winking it over, screwed a redhaired whore.
> Monsignor Capovilla mourned. What a week.
> A journalism doggy took a leak
>
> against absconding coon ('but take one virtue,
> without which a man can hardly hold his own')
> the sun in the willow
> shivers itself & shakes itself green-yellow
> (Abba Pimen groaned, over the telephone,
> when asked what that was:)
>
> How feel a fellow then when he arrive
> in fame but lost? but affable, top-shelf.

Quelle sad semaine.
He hardly know his selving. ('that a man')
Henry grew hot, got laid, felt bad, survived
('should always reproach himself'.

There are two self-contained poems here, one within the paren-
theses, the other outside. They work together in a kind of coun-
terpoint, the words of Abba Pimen on virtue commenting on the
various activities that are described. The statements that Henry
"grew hot" (like the burning Buddhist), got laid (like the Secre-
tary), felt bad (like the Monsignor), and survived (like the ab-
sconding coon) tie the parts of the song together, indicating
Henry's identification with public events, an assumption of responsibility that is possible only if he does indeed reproach himself at all times, the world being what it is. Other aspects of the
poem are also of interest. One is the seemingly irrelevant description of the sun in the middle of the song. Berryman wants to
show the identification of the natural scene—the weeping willow
shining and shaking—with the fouled up world of man. The lines
shift us momentarily from the artificial data of the week in review, providing a glimpse of the enduring reality that makes
them all seem petty. Another nice effect is created by "winking it
over," a play on "thinking it over" that simultaneously suggests
casual indifference and lasciviousness. Berryman was aware that
potential variations and puns hover invitingly over virtually all
words or phrases (especially for one steeped in Joyce) and he
frequently rises to the bait, often with curious results, as in "I
have a sing to shay" (35), "a lessen up your slave" (84); "Harms &
the child I sing" (149).
    A question of some delicacy is raised by the phrase "abscond-
ing coon." Is it defensible for a white poet in the 1960s (or any
other time) to introduce into a work the insulting word "coon,"
or, for that matter, to put his protagonist in blackface and to use

minstrel show dialect? There is a certain amount of naiveté in Berryman's assumption that he could casually employ language that is inflammatory (and it would be inaccurate to refer to such minstrel shows as those performed in the dark ages by the American Legion and Lions Club as anything but racist) without provoking criticism simply because as a man of troubles and griefs he identifies with the black race, glibly taking on its history as his own. Berryman wrote his songs in Minneapolis, where blacks are nearly invisible. His sense of the black experience is clearly derivative, based not on first-hand exposure but on literature. He had, thus, little real understanding of black life, and never, so far as I can determine, encountered black rage. He disliked the South because of its discriminatory practices, yet his experience with the realities of life there was virtually nonexistent. Throughout his career he was protected by his profession and by geography from firsthand knowledge of prejudice and oppression. He spoke with haughty authority about racial issues (as he did about the Vietnamese war) but actually knew little about them. And yet as one reads the songs as objectively as possible it becomes clear that Berryman's feelings of kinship actually are sincere, touchingly so, expressing the self-mockery of a victim, and that if his diction is at times exploitative his motives were nevertheless sound. Convinced that his identification with an oppressed people justified both the disguise and the use of stage dialect, he was, I think, operating in the dark, but his views were clearly well-intended.

Song 95, which begins "The surly cop lookt out at me in sleep / insect-like. Guess, who was the insect," deals with the sort of rage Berryman actually did understand, firsthand. The song, which recounts a bizarre patricidal fantasy, is one of the key works in the book.[12] The allusion to the insect suggests not only "Metamorphosis" but also Kafka's famous letter to his father. The poem introduces an authority figure armed with a pistol who is later referred to as "my guardian." Henry is in a robe and hospital gown, like a sick child. The epithet "meathead" takes on horrifying literal implications, the policeman being cooked and his brains spooned up, the way a child would scoop up strained beef. Henry gets to these brains the same way he gets at his father's casket in number 384, i.e., with his "true & legal ax." This image of a gowned Henry, identifying with Loeb (who murdered calculatingly, in cold blood), and spooning in the brains of his guardian, is as shocking as anything in the book. (It parallels one of the most disturbing images in Tadeusz Borowski's terrifying *This Way for the Gas, Ladies and Gentlemen*, though in Borowski's story the eating is motivated by hunger rather than by rage.) [13] In the last line "the sun flames out," and it is clear that punster Henry is making two points. This time white Henry's rage is real. And the rhetoric is real.

Let me touch on two additional poems that contain within themselves (or derive from the book as a whole) virtually all the information needed for interpretation. Song 123 appears to be somewhat chaotic until one notices that the lines move through a series of associations that have their own sort of logic. The sun on the floor makes Henry think of lying down "to mount a thought." This reminds him (we don't know precisely why) of the *New York Times*, which has a "morgue" full of clippings, used for newsstories and obituaries. This in turn makes him think of the other sort of morgue, and of the ineluctability of death ("c'est la mort"). He will probably die "in underwear," and this image triggers a memory of a woman, "as we met each other once." The poem moves, thus, in the manner of dreams, from sunlight to memory, to the morgue, to dying, then to love, and ends, in a way, where it began. The next song, not surprisingly, celebrates the birth of his son: Henry is delivered "from the gale," and his boy is "out of jail." C'est la vie.

Song 218, "Fortune gave him to know the flaming best," is typical of a rather large number of songs that make their points not by a process of association or through images dredged up from the unconscious but by direct expository statements that conceal no mysteries, and that evoke a purely cerebral response (if any at all). "Expression's kings" (a singularly dull phrase), though never named, are clearly Yeats, Thomas, Eliot, Roethke, Frost (who was two miles away, which means that the song was written during Berryman's Bread Loaf summer), and Lowell, "rugged & grand & sorrowful." The point the poem makes is simply that Henry knew these kings, "by voice & hand." Since name-dropping does not make for much of a song, Berryman tacks on a generalization that is, unfortunately, petulant and hollow:

> Henry as I was muttering knew them man
> by man: much good it did him in his fix
> except for letting out love.

In the "sunlight-underwear" poem, love emerges from the flow of images and associations. Here the word is simply tossed in to resurrect a song that has expired somewhere around the fifth line. Not even love, however, can redeem poetry that is the product not of compelling emotional necessity but of mechanical routine. When Berryman errs on the side of easy generalizations his work invariably goes flat. He is much more effective when he requires his reader to be an imaginative collaborator, when he provides provocative hints and clues rather than bald declarations.

III

The extraordinary technical dexterity demonstrated over and over in the more successful songs reveals just how gifted and versatile a craftsman Berryman was. In moving from the sonnets to

Homage to Mistress Bradstreet he had shifted from one rigidly inhibiting form to another. The "Homage stanza," which has a stress-per-line pattern that goes, with some substitutions, $a^5b^5x^3b^4c^5c^5x^3a^6$ (modelled on Yeats's "In Memory of Major Robert Gregory"), provides little room for flexibility, though Berryman manages to make it seem much less restricting than it actually is. For the dream songs he created a form which, while also quite regular (so that any variations are highlighted), permits even more flexibility, more of the sort of raffishness that he could never resist.

Resembling extended sonnets, the songs are composed of three sections of six lines each, the stanzas separated by white space. There are, within this regular pattern, endless possibilities for variation, and since Berryman has chosen not to close off his options (songs about dreams should, after all, have at least some of the freedom of dreams), virtually any assertion about formal characteristics can be challenged. The one indisputable structural fact is that though no poem has fewer than eighteen lines (or fewer than three stanzas), fifteen go beyond the eighteen, ten songs having one additional line, two having two, and three having three extra lines. While the eighteen-line pattern is plainly the standard on which all structural variations are played, the norm for the work's measure, line by line, is more difficult to determine, the variety being greater, the repeated patterns less predictable. More often than not, however, the words fall into iambs, hundreds of lines being as regular as anything in Frost or Yeats:

He stared at ruin. Ruin stared straight back.

(45)

Supreme my holdings, greater yet my need

(64)

> Scarlatti spurts his wit across my brain,
> So too does *Figaro:* so much for art
>
> (258)
>
> Above the lindens tops of poplars waved
>
> (178)

These are opening lines, chosen pretty much at random. Well over 300 of the songs begin with a pentameter line, and a high percentage of these lines have exactly ten feet. Many of those that are not in pentameter are exact tetrameter or hexameter. Moreover, in nearly every case in which an opening deviates from the iambic norm the second line resolves the tension, falling into exact pentameter, the standard against which the third, invariably much shorter (sometimes made up of only a word or two), is played, thereby achieving its effect. The fourth and fifth lines are more often than not in pentameter, and again, the sixth, imitating the third, is short. This pattern, of shorter third and sixth lines, is generally (but not always) repeated in the second and third stanzas (the stanzas are often mirror images of the first) so that the sense of closure is usually created not by a leisurely pentameter line but by an abrupt statement, often in irregular dimeter or trimeter:

> never take cookies from cats.
>
> (322)
>
> but best is the short day.
>
> (190)
>
> and I will love that touch
>
> (173)
>
> He arose, benign, & performed.
>
> (134)

Song 224 (titled "Eighty"), which is fairly representative, demonstrates some important things about Berryman's rhythmical strategies.

> Lónely in his gréat áge, Hénry's old friénd
> léaned on his búrning cáne while hís old friénd
> was hýmnèd óut of líving.
> The Ábbey ráng with sóund. Póund white as snów
> bówed to thém with his thóughts—it's hárd to knów them thóugh
> for the óld man sáng no wórd.
>
> Drý, rípe with páin, búsy with lóss, let's guéss.
> Góne. Góne them wíne-meetings, góne green grásses
> of the pícnics of rísing youth.
> Góne all, slówly. Státely, nót as the tóngue
> wórries the loóse toóth, wíts as stróng as yoúng,
> ónly the albíno bódy faíling.
>
> Whére the smóther clústers pínpoint ínsights cléar.
> The ténnis is óver. The lást wórds are hére?
> Whát, in the wórld, will they bé?
> Whíte is the húe of déeath & víctory,
> áll the óld generósities dismíssed
> while the whíte yéars insíst.

Considering that ten of the lines have ten syllables one would expect somewhat more regular stress patterns than those I have indicated—and I do not insist that this reading, with its emphasis on thud meter and spondaic substitution, is the only possible one; in several lines (1, 8, and 18 for example) other emphases are equally effective. What is especially absorbing about this song, however, and what accounts for its beauty, is the series of elegant variations wrought within the regular framework. Since the subject is the eighty-year-old Ezra Pound (by now lapsed into silence) at the funeral of his friend T. S. Eliot, it is appropriate that the tone be solemn (Henry represses his usual tendency to play around), the measure deliberate and stately. Each stanza is end stopped, the short final lines slowing the momentum. This retardation is reinforced by the large amount of internal punctuation, especially in stanza two, which gives the poetry a ritualistic quality. After the regular trimeter of line three the extended fourth line ("Pound" must be stressed, as must "white"), with its six stresses, seems to disrupt the majestic regularity of the rhythm, but the tension is partially resolved by the fifth line, also extended, which repeats the six stresses of line five before giving way to the superb monosyllables of line six. This line, in three regular stresses, eloquently resolves the tensions. A similar effect is created in stanza two, where the rhythmically strained eighth line is followed by the perfectly fluid ninth—two anapests and an iamb. The sense of order is, appropriately, most evident in the third stanza, and here it is created by repeated trochees and by the stops at the end of every line except the fifth, which, ending in an atypical iambic word ("dismissed"), flows into the final line in which the momentum is halted by the three insistent stresses that provide closure: white yéars insíst.

The fact that the final stanza is made up of three couplets also helps account for an underlying sense of formal resolution. In stanzas one and two the effects are created largely by internal rhyme, assonance, and alliteration. In the first six lines, for example, "sound-Pound" and "know-though" are the most obvious internal rhymes, but more subtle, more telling, is the response "the old man sang" two lines after "The Abbey rang." The lines have a Miltonic quality, the repetition of the open "o" in particular creating, in a manner that is appropriate to the subject of the song, an organ-like tone: Mourning-Lovely-old-old-snow-bowed-know-though-old-no. The music is continued in the second stanza (loss-slowly-strong-body), and gains a percussive underbeat with the dirge-like repetition of "Gone." There are, finally, a number of image or word contrasts in all three stanzas that eloquently unite the separate parts—sound and silence, grass and snow, growth and age, body and mind. These details, working elegantly with the rhythms and verbal harmonies, communicate a strong sense of loss.

If this song is quite representative of Berryman's rhythmical strategies, it is, in its elaborate formal organization, rather atypical, most of the poems giving the impression (though it is often just that) of a movement more spontaneous, more dreamlike, less deliberately plotted. The book's very first song is more characteristic of certain aspects of Berryman's craft, and merits an analysis.

> Húffy Hénry híd   the dáy,
> Unappeásable Hénry súlked.
> I sée his póint,—a trýing to pút things óver.
> Ít was the thóught that they thóught
> they could *dó* it máde Hénry wícked & awáy.
> But he shóuld have come óut and tálked.
>
> Áll the wórld like a woólen lóver
> ónce did seém on Hénry's síde.
> Thén cáme a depárture.
> Thereáfter nóthing fell óut as it míght or óught.
> I dón't sée how Hénry, príed
> ópen for áll the wórld to sée, survíved.
>
> Whát he has nów to sáy is a lóng
> wónder the wórld can béar & bé.
> Ónce in a sýcamore I was glád
> Áll at the tóp, and I sáng.
> Hárd on the lánd wéars the stróng séa
> And émpty grows évery béd.

Again, the stanzas are self-contained, but the rhythms are more complex, and the norm on which the variations are played is the four- rather than five-stress line. The sound pattern is also more subtle, the strong regular rhymes (day-away, thought-ought, etc.)

partly obscuring the less obtrusive slant rhymes (sulked-talked, long-sang, glad-bed).

With its alliterative opening phrase followed by a caesura the first line resembles Anglo-Saxon verse, except that the half line following the pause fails to repeat the pattern of the first half. It is clear that the repetition of the "h" sound is meant to underscore the implications of "huffy." The pause, however, where one would logically expect a preposition, such as "throughout," thus making a conventional five-stress line, lets the reader know immediately that he must collaborate actively, must suspend his expectations and learn to hear Henry's music. After the comically alliterative expression of persecution ("the thought that they thought"), Henry describes himself (the "I" and "his" being the same person) as "wicked & away." This odd phrase, totally unexpected, is quintessential Berryman, the sort of thing that accounts, at least in part, for the charm of Henry's lengthy lamentation.

The transition between the first stanza and the second is implicit rather than obvious: we immediately discover why Henry is in such a rotten mood. The world was once on his side, like a woolen lover, which suggests someone wrapped in a warm blanket, sharing Henry's side of the bed (and the empty bed emerges explicitly at the song's end). Following the departure, and the ensuing disappointment, Henry introduces the image of being "pried open." There are several possible interpretations for this phrase. It suggests, for one thing, an oyster, pried open for its pearl—and "all the world" was Henry's oyster once. (In number 25 he is referred to as "valved.") It also suggests the scene of number 91 in which, like Lazarus, Henry is dug up from a grave. And "pried open" implies, in addition, an operation, a reading that takes on added resonance when we come to number 67, in which Henry conducts operations of great delicacy on his own body. (In number 8, another hospital poem, "They lifted off / his

covers till he showed, and cringed & pled.") The word "pry"
also hints at secrets, knowledge of intimate details, and as a poet
Henry has been, and still is, on display, his "pride" in his "long
wonder" subject to the world's scrutiny. The world, however, no
longer a single lover, is now a manipulative, impersonal "they."

While in stanza two Henry does not understand how he survived, he introduces in the final stanza an elegiac lament for past
happiness—the memory of what has been and never more will
be—when he sang like a bird in a tree. This image, which derives
from references in the *Sonnets* to the sycamore outside Lise's
house (and which may also allude to Zacchaeus in a tree, watching Christ pass),[14] is picked up in the final song in the first book:
"The glories of the world struck me, made me aria, once," and
later, in number 352, "He sang on like a harmful bird," as well as
elsewhere. The concluding lines have considerable power. In the
course of the songs we come to associate the sea both with Berryman's mother (and birth) and with his father (and death). In this
case the "empty bed," following the sexual pun in "hard on,"
looks back specifically to the departed woolen lover as well as
generally to attrition (the sea wearing down the land) and to loss
through death. Moreover, the movement from the singing bird to
the empty bed is related to the image in number 68 of Pinetop
and Charlie (Bird) Parker playing the "Empty Bed" blues.

This song, putting forth images of a man sulking alone (like
Achilles when his bedmate has been taken from him), of a woolen
lover, of a prying open, a sycamore, and finally of the sea and an
empty bed, introduces its symbols with the associational logic of a
dream. It is helpful when reading the songs to remember that
dreams (including nightmares), on which so many of them are
modelled, are mysterious, that they tend to lack coherent transitions, and that their symbols are often grotesquely distorted. To
explain away particularly difficult passages, however, by saying
that dreams are, after all, inscrutable, would be to give up our

critical and imaginative prerogatives too easily. Dreams (and songs, and poets) can be analyzed, if not always definitively, then at least suggestively. Moreover, there are a great many songs (the one describing Pound at Eliot's funeral, for example) that have nothing to do with dreams. A few, some quite wonderful (101, 317), are apparently transcriptions of dreams, but these are outnumbered by those in which dreamwork, if involved at all, comprises only one facet of the song.

The caesura in line one, the ampersand in line five ("wicked & away"), the complex interlacing of rhymes, the repeated word ("Henry" is named five times in eleven lines), and the images picked up in other songs are all strategies that Berryman employs throughout the book. There are, of course, many other characteristic rhetorical devices as well. One of Henry's favorites is the creation of descriptive epithets for himself, e.g. "The Man Who Did Not Deliver" (43), "a cagey John" (51), "the brain from hell" (9). He also employs personification, as in "General Fatigue stalked in" (93). He likes to put the ballad-syllable "O" at the beginning or end of a line, usually as much in the interests of rhythmical regularity as of picturesque speech, e.g. "My flaskie O, / O crystal cock" (64). He uses the rhythms and diction of blues and nursery songs. He delights, as I have indicated, in puns, some quite simple ("Back to lurk!"), others more elaborate ("The more I lessen to, the bore I hears"). He likes the zeugma, e.g., "saved by his double genius & certain emendations," or "With a large Jameson & a worse hangover." He frequently refers to other writers by name, and also works into the sequence a number of echoes, from Donne, Yeats, Cummings, the Bible, Hopkins, Kafka, Tennyson, Owen, Shakespeare, and many others.

Like his speaker in the sonnets (and like the practitioners of the French "New" Novel) Berryman also several times alludes to his own work in progress, particularly as the sequence moves toward its conclusion. These passages make up a small body of critical comment which, though it discourages analysis by authors of interpretive studies, is very winning. Henry's attitude toward his own work, as much as his quest for religious certainty, his Weltanschauung, or his desire to forgive himself, becomes a central subject of the book:

> Why then did he make, at such cost, *crazy* sounds?
> to waken ancient longings, to remind (of childness),
> to make laugh, and to hurt,
> is and was all he ever intended.
>
> (271)

> What gall had he in him, so to begin Book VII
> or to design, out of its hotspur materials,
> its ultimate structure
> whereon will critics browse at large, at Heaven Eleven
>
> (293)

> My baby chatters. I feel the end is near
> & strong of my large work, which will appear,
> and baffle everybody.
> They'll seek the strange soul, in rain & mist,
> whereas they should recall the pretty cousins they kissed,
> and stick with the sweet switch of the body.
>
> (308, "An Instructions to Critics")

> These Songs are not meant to be understood, you understand.
> They are only meant to terrify & comfort.
>
> (366)

> will assistant professors become associates
> by working on his works?
>
> (373)

It is clear that Berryman-Henry is eager to delight and comfort, to make laugh, as well as to terrify and to hurt. The delight and laughter result, in large part, from the charm of his language which, when colorful and inventive, as it often is, can be irresistible—though I am aware that one man's picturesque quirkiness may well be another man's nonsense. I am thinking of such things as "wicked & away," in which normal diction is fractured just enough to create an original effect but not so much as to distort or destroy the meaning. Henryspeech, that queer language peculiar to this work, derives its effects from archaic and Latinate constructions, from crumpled syntax, odd diction, idiomatic conversation, and conscious violation of grammatical rules ("I like it so less I don't understood"; "My madnesses have cease"). Even the reader willing to accept this playing around on Henry's own terms will probably be put off now and then by Berryman's tendency to be cute, by verbal confusion, and by excesses of various sorts, but he is almost certain also to be won over by phrases, or passages, that are fresh and memorable. Let me give a few examples of the sort of thing I think works well. Song 6, which deals in part with father-son conflicts, ends with the line "these grapes of stone were being proferred, friend," a nice modernization (the "proferred" providing a self-ironic, highfalutin' tone) of the Biblical verse "In all ages the fathers have eaten of the bitter grapes, and the sons' teeth were put on edge." "So many, some / won't find a rut to park" Henry says in song 10, describing a lovers' area filled with cars. By using "rut" rather than the expected "place" or "spot" he underscores the animalistic purposes of the trysting-place. "Toddlers are taking over" (12), is a splendidly succinct summary of the rise of a new generation into power. "You can biff me, you can bang me, get it you'll never. / I may be only a Polack   broad but I don't lay easy" (15), is a direct transcription of language (used by a woman "haughty & greasy") heard by Bellow in a Chicago bar, according to Dr. Thomes, and passed along to Berryman. It is reminiscent of the unembellished vernacular talk heard by Williams in his house calls and worked into his poems. In number 34 we get a colorful synopsis of Hemingway as writer, sportsman, and lover:

he verbed for forty years, very enough,
& shot & buckt—and, baby, there was of
schist but small there (some).

Robert Frost is summarized as "the quirky medium of so many
truths" (38), and of Stevens Henry says "Mutter we all must as
well as we can. / He mutter spiffy" (219). "I doubt he'll make / old
bones" (43) is his way of saying he won't live to an old age. A
bull, in Zaragoza, is "willing not to die" (62). "My kneel has gone
to seed" (64) is how Henry describes his loss of faith. Asked why
he has been drinking for two decades running, his answer is neat
and to the point: "Man, I been thirsty" (96). He can sum up in a
phrase what generations of academics have thought but ne'er so
well expressed: "All over the world grades are being turned in,
/ and isn't that a truly gloomy thought" (176). "I read the 'paper
gingerly lest I grieve" (203) says troubled Henry, and "I
should   have been a noted crook / or cat in a loud slum yes"
(343).

The flaws in the songs generally result either from a dormant
imagination (so that the language sounds tired rather than newly
minted) or from a reaching for an effect that doesn't quite come
off. Even the most brilliant talkers, like Schwartz, or Lowell, or
Berryman himself, occasionally fall below their most dazzling
levels, and it is not surprising to find in a work of nearly four
hundred pages some lapses in intensity and invention. Particularly in the sequence in which Delmore Schwartz is eulogized inspiration seems to fail, and this suggests that Berryman was able
to deal more eloquently with general sorrow, especially involving
himself, than with a specific loss. The tone tends to be flat and
petulant rather than deeply felt, e.g., "This world is gradually
becoming a place / where I do not care to be any more" (149), or
"my tearducts are worn out" (151), or, in spite of the pun, weakest of all, "I'm cross with god." (The poem, number 153, which

begins so badly, ends on a note of understatement that helps save it: "And never again can come, like a man slapped, / news like this.") The opening of number 155 is singularly inappropriate, an embarrassing example of witless wit: "I can't get him out of my mind, out of my mind, / Hé was out of his mind for years." In number 157 Schwartz is described (by a poet who despised clichés) as a "first-rate soul." Examples of dull or obvious word-play also show up here and there elsewhere in the book. Henry's arm, for example, is "fractured in the humerus: no joke to Henry, nothing humorous," and the line lies down and dies of exhaustion.

Since the seven books that make up the work are at best occasionally flawed and at worst extremely uneven, every reader is likely to become his or her own godlike editor, identifying those songs that should definitely be included in a slimmed-down version of the book. My own view is that a rather large number, particularly in Books V and VI, perhaps as many as fifty in all, could be dropped without any great loss to the overall work. *The Dream Songs* gets off to a stunning beginning, the first fifty songs being, line by line, richer, denser, and more complex than any other comparable section. Books III and IV, if not so consistently brilliant as the first two, maintain a high level. The fifth book, with some notable exceptions, shows a marked falling off. Things improve in VI, the longest of the sections, which contains a large number of superb pages as well as many that are relatively flat and loose, the density of imagery in the early sections replaced by an easier prosiness. Book VII is the most unified, the most novelistic, and in many ways, especially in its combination of lucidity and eloquence, the strongest of the sections. It completes the poem in a fashion worthy of its remarkable opening.

I would suggest (with understandable trepidation) that the following are the most expendable of the songs, and that their exclusion would make the book as a whole leaner, tougher, more consistently fine.

II #32 And where, friend Quo, lay you hiding

III #59 Down on the cathedrals, as from the Giralda
     #73 The taxi makes the vegetables fly.

IV #99 He does not live here but it *is* the god.
    #102 The sunburnt terraces which swans make home
    #116 Through the forest, followed, Henry made his silky way.
    #120 Foes I sniff, when I have less to shout
    #138 Henry, moot, grunted. Like a lily of the valley

VI #183 Eastward he longs, before, well, any bad
    #188 There is a kind of undetermined hair,
    #196 I see now all these deaths are to one end—
    #218 Fortune gave him to know the flaming best,
    #221 I poured myself out thro' my tips. What's left?
    #243 An undead morning. I . . . shuffle my poss's.
    #244 Calamity Jane lies very still
    #245 Find me a sur-vivid fool, find me another
    #247 Henry walked as if he were ashamed
    #248 Snowy of her breasts the drifts, I do believe,
    #262 The tenor of the line of your retreats,
    #270 This fellow keeps on sticking at his drum,
    #273 Survive—exist—who is at others' will

VII #288 In the neighbourhoods evil of noise, he deployed, Henry,
    #291 Cold & golden lay the high heroine
    #312 I have moved to Dublin to have it out with you,
    #321 O land of Connolly & Pearse, what have
    #324 Henry in Ireland to Bill underground:

There are phrases, lines, and even passages in these poems that are splendid, but the songs themselves, either because they are obvious, or rhythmically dull, or excessively obscure, or because (as in the case of "Calamity Jane lies dead") they seem to belong in another book, detract from the power of the work. Would not such deletions, however, interfere with the movement and thematic coherence of the individual sections, not to mention the organizational integrity of the work as a whole? I do not think so. Berryman did not have anyone to do for *The Dream Songs* what Pound did for (and to) *The Waste Land,* nor did he, like Whitman, continue to revise and edit his song of himself after its initial publication. The work, put bluntly, is padded, and though a sequence must have "dull patches" as a relief from brilliance, any reader-editor, hearing the 385 songs over and over, will begin to identify those that add little or nothing to the overall conception.

Following up on this question of the individual parts that contribute to the whole, I want to focus on each of the seven sections to isolate dominant themes. I will also comment, in the process, on any significant organizational patterns, such as groups of songs or linked songs. As I have already pointed out, the first book opens with Henry undergoing a paranoid sulk, and closes twenty-five songs later with a symbolic death. This opening section functions like an overture, presenting motifs that are later varied and developed. It also introduces the two central characters, Henry, whose "I," "his," and "he," become, at the end of the first song, simply "I," and his pal, "Tambo," [15] who first appears in the second song. Twenty-one of the songs are Henry's solos, and five are duets, or dialogues. In three of these Tambo expresses a point of view, faintly censorious, and in the others he impersonates Mr. Interlocutor, raising questions ("—Wha happen then, Mr. Bones?") for Henry to answer.

Numerous themes are introduced in this opening section. We find in number 18, "A Strut for Roethke," the first of the several eulogies for dead friends. There are references, explicit and implicit, to Henry's dead father, to blindness, and to Henry's dislike of himself, e.g. "Henry bores me" (14), "Henry was not his favourite" (15). Other motifs are also introduced: fame, the contrast between past and present (the reel of childhood films becoming "real"), identification with criminals, the capacity to hurt others, envy of the dead, castration fears. The phrase "It's golden here in the snow" in number 9 and the menacing bears in number 11 introduce motifs that weave in and out of all seven books.

Three themes in this first book are of particular importance, and they are, in crucial ways, related to one another: mortality, lust, and a preoccupation with religion. The latter is especially significant, "God," "Heaven," "hell," or "the Lord" playing a part in over a third of the songs. Though Henry has lost the faith of his youth (his kneel having gone to seed) he has lost neither his thirst for grace nor his obsession with the creator of this insane planet—toward the end of his life Berryman returned to the Catholicism of his childhood, and at the time of his death he was planning to write a life of Christ for children. At odds with his God, he has become a kind of "ornery" Lucifer who knows that "God's Henry's enemy" (13). He is also, nevertheless, involved in a strenuous spiritual quest, and in his efforts to exorcise his evil lodger has sought out Luther, St. Simeon (a Syrian ascetic), and Baal Shem Tov (the founder of Chassidism, a sect of Jewish mystics in Poland). Henry is aware that the more sin increases "the more / grace has been caused to abound," and is still able to turn to his God, whether out of habit or with real hope, in supplication. The single most pervasive literary source for these opening songs is John Donne. In number 13, Henry pleads "Come & diminish me, & map my way," a variation on "whilst my Physitians by their love are growne / Cosmographers, and I their mapp." Number 17 begins, "Muttered Henry:—Lord of matter, thus; / upon some more unquiet spirit knock," an echo of Donne's powerful "Batter my heart, three person'd God. . . ."

A most curious Christian reference is found in Song 21. After describing the "senior population" in their graves ("Come down! come down!") Henry tells of an "ancient man" in a madhouse who mutters " 'O come on down. O come on down.' / Clear whom *he* meant." The implication is that anyone who looks for the second coming must be mad.[16] One gets the impression, however, that Henry is not so sure. He himself, of course, is not "ancient" (he is in his early fifties), but he is "Bones," mortal and aging. He sees toddlers taking over, speaks of "a teenage cancer, with a plan," (22), and sees himself as "old, old" (7). This helps account, at least in part, for the urgency with which he attempts to attain some sort of faith.

In "A Stimulant for an Old Beast" (3), Henry is clearly the beast. The beauty is "screwed-up lovely 23." Death is clearly the mother of desire, and Henry's sexual obsession, already strong, is increased by his heightened awareness of his own physical decline. Like Rilke, whom he mentions, he is especially attracted to young women. In the delightful fourth song, "Filling her compact & delicious body," our hero, virtually fainting with desire, comes close to "springing on her" (like an old beast), but has to be content with his spumoni. "There ought to be a law against Henry," Henry moans, and his friend assures him "—Mr. Bones: there is." In his final song of the section, Tambo asks Mr. Bones why he no longer arias, and the response: "Henry. Henry became interested in women's bodies." His lust causes Henry to fall back into "the original crime: art, rime." Thus at this early stage of his narrative it is not wine but women and song that account for the chaos in Henry's life.

In the second book (or section) the central ideas of section one are further developed, and new themes are introduced. Twenty-one of the songs are solos, and Tambo shows up in four, twice to raise questions and twice to make typically deflating comments. Just as the wicked "Lay of Ike" provides comic relief in the first section, the song about the Modern Language Association (35) evokes some satirical chuckles in the midst of a group of poems about death. And it is the subject of death, even more than religion, that dominates this section. The single eulogy on Roethke in the first book expands now to a cluster, one on Hem-

ingway (34), another, 36 ("The high ones die, die") on Hemingway and Faulkner "(Frost being still around)," immediately followed by three on Frost (37, 38, and 39). Number 41 deals with
the deaths of animals and men "(and Death is a German expert),"
and number 42 is addressed to his dead father ("Fate winged me,
in the person of a cab / and your stance on the sand"), also
present in the Hemingway poem, i.e., "whose sire as mine one
same way." In number 48 Henry is still "full of the death of
love," and in number 49 his waking is "like death." The section
begins with Henry asserting "I'll die." It is little wonder that the
final song contains a plea: "spare now a cagey John / a whilom bits
that whip."

The Christian imagery continues to assume a major role, especially in number 47, "April Fool's Day, or, St Mary of Egypt,"
and number 48, with its play on bread "rising in the Second Gospel," crust, and eating. The song finds Henry "mourning / the
whole implausible necessary thing," which suggests that in spite
of his doubts about Christ (he has by now become an "imaginary
Jew") he desperately needs the assurances of his youth. Number
46 is a charming allegory on the redeeming power of faith, which
eventually dies, to be followed by "other deaths." While these
poems are relatively impersonal, "Snow Line" (number 28),
which just precedes "There sat down, once, a thing on Henry's
heart," is a more intimate revelation of Berryman's spiritual long-
ings.

> It was wet & white & swift and where I am
> we don't know. It was dark and then
> it isn't.
> I wish the barker would come. There seems to be to eat
> nothing. I am unusually tired.
> I'm alone too.
>
> If only the strange one with so few legs would come,
> I'd say my prayers out of my mouth, as usual.

Where are his notes I loved?
There may be horribles; it's hard to tell.
The barker nips me but somehow I feel
he too is on my side.

I'm too alone. I see no end. If we could all
run, even that would be better. I am hungry.
The sun is not hot.
It's not a good position I am in.
If I had to do the whole thing over again
I wouldn't.

What is the whole thing? Life? Departure from God? Separation
from the fold? The poet obviously keeps matters ambiguous in-
tentionally, but we can nevertheless see that the song gives a persuasive description of the anxiety that comes with a state of sin
(and this is not the "chortle sin" of number 57), an anxiety utterly
impossible to live with. Henry adopts the symbolic role of lost
sheep, hungry, alone, and cold. In simple, childlike language he
longs for the good shepherd (the strange one with so few legs)
and his dog (the barker). The litotes of "It's not a good position I
am in" adds to the moving simplicity of this odd and somehow affecting song, certainly one of the key poems in the second book.

In book three, songs 59–77, images of blindness, aging, and
"the thing" reappear, and several new motifs assume some importance. Henry's new wife, for example, prepared for in the second book ("he's about to have his lady, permanent") appears,
with their son, in three songs, numbers 54, 56, and 67. Images of
alcohol are present here and there, generally in a minor way ("a
martini strangely needed," "my flaskie O," "Feeling no pain,"
"Bafflin odd sobriety"), but with sufficient frequency to prepare
for the delirium tremens of the later books. The lecherous yearning so powerful in section one all but disappears (there is, after
all, a new young wife), though it does resurface in one comic
poem (69), easy and light, that is to this section what the "Ike"
and "MLA" songs are to the first and second:

> —Vouchsafe me, Sleepless One,
> a personal experience of the body of Mrs Boogry
> before I pass from lust!

Tambo plays an important role in this section, speaking in seven songs, of which number 60 is of particular interest. In a dialogue with liberal Henry, who is offended by the failure of the South to integrate, Tambo assumes the role of an Uncle Tom, pointing out "is coloured officers, / Mr Bones. Dat's nuffin?" After suggesting that the moans of the "ofays" are "brownin up to ourn," he asks Henry who will win, and the response: "—I wouldn't *pre*dict. / But I do guess mos peoples gonna *lose*." Song 68 also has racial discrimination as its theme. Henry, in a dream, performs on stage (the song is "Yellow Dog") with Bessie Smith, until "she totterin," and then "we wait and see." At this point "Empty Bed" is played:

> they all come hangin Christmas on some tree
> after trees thrown out—sick-house's white birds',
> black to the birds instead.

In other words, praise comes too late. And the hospital is for whites only; blacks are told to go to the birds. Bessie Smith, denied admission, died in her car.

If this lament contains an implicit allusion to "Bye Bye Blackbird," another popular song emerges outright in number 76. It follows "Henry's confession," when, after saying that life is a handkerchief sandwich, that is, a place of no sustenance but many tears, he asserts:

> in a modesty of death I join my father
> who dared so long agone leave me.
> A bullet on a concrete stoop
> close by a smothering southern sea
> spreadeagled on an island, by my knee.

Tambo suggests that the two walk arm in arm "by the beautiful sea" and that Mr Bones hum. Instead of singing "You and me, you and me, Oh how happy we'd be," Henry says, simply, "I saw nobody coming, so I went instead." This distressing description of his father's leaving (with its archaic "agone" suggesting agony) should be read in the context of number 54, in which Henry, shot "full of sings," in his hospital room, thinks of his beloved poet Issa and his father who "sat down on the grass and took leave of each other." [17]

As I suggest earlier, Henry's revelation about his father's death serves a valuable therapeutic function, giving way as it does to the section's final song in which we find him in Fall, awake, shaved, duded up, and, having swung his barbells, ready to move on. This mellow poem indicates a recovery that is physical as well as emotional, many of the earlier songs (like that about Issa) being set in a hospital. In the opening song of book three, "Bright-eyed . . . woke not Henry up." By the final poem his eyes are "ancient fires."

He is also "impenitent," a far cry from the questing sinner of numbers 55, 56, and 57, who mourns the death of his faith. The first of these "quest" poems is quite accessible. It "seems to take place after Henry's death," Berryman said in a tape-recorded reading. [18] Henry is apparently at heaven's gate being interviewed by St. Peter. Things, helped by martinis, go well until a chill falls, he feels his application failing, and another sound is heard. A voice, which may be Christ's, asserts "We betrayed me." The next song, number 56, descending from heaven to hell, is somewhat more complex. It begins:

> Hell is empty. O that has come to pass
> which the cut Alexandrian foresaw,
> and Hell lies empty.
> Lightning fell silent where the Devil knelt
> and over the whole grave space hath settled awe
> in a full death of guilt.

This is something that Henry would like desperately to accept as true. The Alexandrian is Origen, a Christian philosopher and teacher in Alexandria (A.D. 185?–254?), "cut" because he castrated himself, adhering literally to the idea that if the eye offends it should be plucked out. Henry wants to believe, with this philosopher, that God, being love, cannot maintain sinners in hell forever, and hence that ultimate salvation (and the death of guilt) is inevitable.

The religious brooding continues in the next poem, which falls neatly into halves. In the first part Henry asks whether his "state of chortle sin" (a pun on mortal sin) will take him to hell, and then, in a Miltonic echo, asserts that hell doesn't exist "save sullen here, wherefrom she flies tonight." He then remembers a treed coon, seen at midnight when he was seven, with which he identified so completely that "I was in that tree." At the end of the song Henry says "I fell out of the tree." This clearly symbolizes his fall from innocence, from grace, into sin. (It also looks back to the loss, in number 1, of the Eden-like sycamore.) And there is the awareness that, like the stag killed in the song just preceding, the coon will be set upon by dogs and killed.

In number 53 Henry describes a novelist "hot as a firecracker" (probably Bellow) who identifies with everything in the newspapers, including corpses. Henry himself is burdened with this sort of sensibility, empathizing not only with the coon but with dead soldiers who lie with mouldered toes, disarmed (61), with a frightened rabbit (62), bats (63), a burning Buddhist (66), Bessie Smith (68), and with his dead father. He is like Williams' Noah Paterson, containing within his own skin all sorts of living things, male and female, human and wild. In one of the section's crucial poems, moreover, number 75, the first of those in which Henry comments on his own work, this seedy hero even joins the vegetable world, putting forth a book that is in fact an "unshedding bulky bole-proud blue-green moist" thing that over the years loses only a few leaves. This time the dogs are critics, who "drew closer for a second look / and performed their friendly operations there." The song ends exuberantly with the description of the effect on passers-by of this marvelous thing made by "savage & thoughtful / surviving Henry," the "flashing & bursting tree!" These atypical affirmative lines prepare us for the seedy Henry of the final poem, stripped down, in fall, and ready to move on.

The fourteen songs of book four, each subtitled "Op. posth." comprise a unified block of communications received from Henry's coffin. The usual meaning of "posthumous," published after death, is extended to mean *composed* after death. (The Latin word, deriving from *postumus,* superlative of *posterus,* "coming after," was influenced by *humus,* earth, taken as "after burial.") The songs show a preoccupation with the decline and decay of the body: Henry's "parts were fleeing," "I'm collapsing," "I am breaking up." His mind, or soul, lives on, taking a detached interest in the disappearance of the body, actually relieved to be rid of the physical ordeal, hoping that it too, the spirit or mind, can be put properly to rest so that it will not, like the ghost of Hamlet's father, "freeze our blood / with terrible returns." The idea of resurrection, however, of returning from the grave, is insistent, cropping up in the second, sixth, tenth (especially), and twelfth songs. The theme also surfaces, of course, in the remarkable fourteenth song, in which Henry is literally dug up. These songs, which foreshadow his return, prepare us for the nearly three hundred lyrics that follow.

The fourteen "Op. posth." poems constitute a link, a transition, and a needed change of pace between the first three books and the last three. They raise questions about whether seedy Henry will continue putting forth leaves, and if so, why? They were clearly written during a period of severe physical decline, probably in a hospital, during which Berryman felt that his body was literally fleeing and that, alert in mind as he was, he would probably be unable to continue his work. He was impelled to fantasize

about his death, his obituaries, the worms at his corpse, his sub-
terranean sex life, his posthumous reputation, his uneasy spirit,
and his resurrection. The reason he is unable simply to be content on his flat back in "the *nice* pit," the "cozy grave," is
revealed in the sixth song, in which "no typewriters—ha! ha!" is
followed by "no typewriters-/ alas!" The reason for the regrets?

> For I have much to open, I know immense
> troubles & wonders to their secret curse.
> Yet when erect on my ass,
>
> pissed off, I sat two-square, I kept shut his mouth
> and stilled my nimble fingers across keys.
> That is I stood up.
>
> Now since down I lay, void of love & ruth,
> I'd howl my knowings, only there's the earth
> overhead. Plop!

One is conditioned to be solemn about graveyard poetry, to
maintain a decorous, funereal face. And these songs, after all, are
about death and decay, about the loss of love, about Dylan &
Randall, so we are likely to approach them reverently, in whis-
pers. The sequence, however, except for the eleventh and thirteenth songs, invites a quite different response, that of amuse-
ment, the merriment deriving not merely from some minor
gallows humor but from a comic blending of diction and tone.
Moreover, there is something essentially risible, after all, about
the spectacle of a melodramatic narcissist moaning and groaning
about his decline, his fleeing parts, his helpless tenement. The
obvious hyperbole permits the reader to keep his emotional distance. Berryman, I think, expects us to apply the corrective of
laughter to the excessive laments.

In the lines quoted above, for example, "erect on my ass" and
"pissed off" should be sufficient to deflate any solemn lugubrious-
ness. Toward the end of the passage Henry does get earnest, as-

serting that now that he is unable to write he would "howl" his knowings. Lest this new tone carry the day, however, he concludes "only there's the earth / overhead. Plop!" Poems that end with a plop do not generally engage our most serious attention. Nor do those that so begin, and to make sure that no one misses the point, Berryman opens the next song "Plop, plop. The lobster toppled in the pot."

In the second of the songs, which contains the serious message that Henry's restless spirit may return if he is not given his day of mourning, both the inflated epic questions ("was sandalwood in good supply when he / flared out of history") and the involvement of the "bulging cosmos" in "heroic" Henry's death operate on a level of lampoon that is engaging. Number 8 finds Henry squirming in his hole, and his wood (read "Henry House") seems to be rotting. He vitiates the gothic grotesqueries of the scene, however, with the comic stiff-upper-lip of "I daresay I'm collapsing." In number 12 the dark humor of the second stanza gives way to a quite moving final stanza, followed, in turn, by the serious thirteenth song. In the second stanza Henry likens his coffin to Grand Central Station, a crowd of women joining him in marriage, with vows rasped and rings exchanged—though these spectral brides must leave with the "lapse of light" when wandering spirits return to their own graves. The stanza ends with a question, "Which one will waken him?" and the song concludes:

> O she must startle like a fallen gown,
> content with speech like an old sacrament
> in deaf ears lying down,
> blazing through darkness till he feels the cold
> & blindness of his hopeless tenement
> while his black arms unfold.

The delicacy of the imagery, and the rich aural harmonies, especially in the "o" sounds, give the potentially bizarre final image a

luminous solemnity—it is a stunning portrayal of the beginnings
of rejuvenation brought about by a woman who combines physical magnetism with lucid intelligence. Given the nearly sacred
tone of the stanza, the double rhyme, sacrament-tenement,
which in another context might lapse into doggerel, becomes one
with the other moving effects.

In the final song the rhymes are clearly *meant* to create a
basically comic tone. The Byronic "Solitude" and "though, now,
glued" would do the job even without the Eliotic "taxes"–"Axis,"
also in the second stanza, and when these are complemented by
"2 a.m."–"strategem" it is clear that while no newsman will unravel Henry's plan, any reader can solve Berryman's, which is to
end the section on a note of cynical levity, a mode that in no way
suggests final closure. Henry will go on, in hundreds of songs,
seeking some sort of peace above the sod. This suggestion of con-
tinuity is, as I have mentioned, made most explicitly in the tenth
song, which is actually the final half of a double poem, the last
line of number nine carrying over to the opening of number ten.
Together these songs comprise the key statement in the section,
summing up Henry's past achievement ("He spiced us," "incapable of crime save salt/preservative"), his present situation ("Not
Guilty by reason of death"), and his future ("Henry may be returning to our life"). He has no "lessen up his slave," but he
clearly intends to "freeze our blood / with terrible returns."

There are a few lines in these fourteen poems that are ambiguous. Is the "house-guest" (in number 3), "daughter of a friend,"
his third wife? Does she represent "bits of outer God?" Is the
"little" meant to suggest Twissy? Is she the descendant of "the
abominable & semi-moral Cat?" What have "Political Econ-
omy" and "military establishments" (number 7) to do with "re-
lishy bodies?" What is the order Henry obeys in number 11?
These puzzles tease the imagination. If the lines are baffling,
however, they detract very little from the overall achievement of

this pivotal block of poems—bizarre, moving, largely coherent, and, God bless Henry, wildly funny.

Book five begins in "Room 231" (in a hospital) where Henry, still as his cadaver, with eyes bleared west ("I am headed west," he announces in Op. posth. no. 13) is waking to march. The song, a conscious variation on Sylvia Plath's "Tulips," also set in a hospital, represents a recovery from the horizontal posture of the "posthumous" book. This new section, which ends with his father's death (leaving Henry "to-live on"), contains fifty-three songs, more than any two of the earlier books combined. Unfortunately only a few of these (and I would single out numbers 95, 101, 123, 129, 135, 142, 143, and 145) are on a par with the best work of the other sections.

If less brilliant, however, the book is nevertheless of a piece, dramatically and thematically, with those that precede it. Tambo shows up seven times, though he is absent for a long stretch before reappearing for the conclusion. He is very much in character throughout, e.g., "Mr Bones, / stop that damn dismal" (98); "Mr Bones, you strong on moral these days, hey?" (142). The book's themes are by now familiar: alcohol, children, teaching, fame, hospital musings (the first five songs are set in a hospital), and madness. A new minor motif is introduced in a cluster of songs commemorating special occasions, New Year's Day (103) and the birthdays of his mother (100), his "Lady" (112), and Shakespeare (97). In number 104 he celebrates his own fifty-first birthday:

> O love,
> what was you loafing of
> that fifty put you off, out & away,
> leaving the pounding, horrid sleep by day,
> nights naught but fits.

Another new motif involves matters quite outside Henry's interior world, touching on persons or events familiar to him, but described in such a way as to remain, for the reader, obscure. Number 110, for example, may be either a terrible dream or may concern the actual drowning of a child. Those involved in the "crime" go uncharged, by the generally intimidating New York Police Force, and continue to run a laundry. The phrase "Now Teddy was hard on" is baffling. Another song, number 115, apparently not a dream poem, touches on a neglected and rejected writer, indifferent to her literary fate, who works in a Great Neck bakery. There is no way of determining who she is, and the main interest in this exceedingly odd poem (what, for example, is a "7-foot weed"?) rests in Henry's response to her situation.

Similar in their baffling references but much more suggestive, in that the imagery invites collaborative response, are the songs that clearly transcribe dreams: these include numbers 101, 111, 116, and 137. The first, for example, finds Henry showing his mother around a lunatic asylum where the inmates never leave their cells, and where a policeman trundles a siren up a walk. The closing stanza evokes "the thing" on Henry's heart of book one:

> I can't go into the meaning of the dream
> except to say a sense of total LOSS
> afflicted me thereof:
> an absolute disappearance of continuity & love
> and children away at school, the weight of the cross,
> and everything is what it seems.

Assuming that everything "seems" unbearable, the weight of the final line, as of the cross Henry bears, is great. Why these particular images, such as Don calling down " 'a drink' / while showering," produce this depression remains mysterious to the reader, as we assume it does to Henry, but we are able, because of the authority of the presentation, to accept the validity of his feelings.

As the treatment of loss and of "the cross" suggests, the section continues the elaboration on the subjects that most engage

Henry's attention, his anger with and quest for God and his obsession with death. Henry's quarrel with God—and with himself—has primarily to do with the deaths of those close to him, and now in this fifth book it is Randall Jarrell and, as in the others, his father who account for his pity, fear, and anger. When Henry says, in the first song, "empty grows every bed," he is referring not only to the loss of a lover but to the disappearance of an extraordinarily large number of his peers. It is a source of guilt and sorrow to Henry (read Berryman) that he, who longs to be in his grave, should have survived the harvest that carried off Jarrell, Schwartz, Blackmur, Winters, Roethke, Thomas, Plath, Hemingway, and Faulkner. Bellow lives, and Lowell, but somehow they are, like Berryman himself, lonely survivors of the plague, or, to shift the image, they are those whose open boats somehow managed to make it to shore. Already preoccupied with his father's unceremonious disappearance, Henry is unable to understand how he has endured, or why God has taken those like Jarrell who, as it happens, was exactly Berryman's age:

> Grief is fatiguing. He is out of it,
> the whole humiliating Human round,
> out of this & that.
>
> (121)
>
> His friend's death had been adjudged suicide,
> which dangles a trail
>
> longer than Henry's chill, longer than his loss
>
> (127)

Painful as this is, it is still less difficult for Henry to come to terms with Jarrell's death by suicide than with the squalid "natural" death, in a run-down hotel, of his gifted and alcoholic friend Delmore Schwartz. After ending book five with a three-song sequence on his father, Henry opens book six with a block of ten poems eulogizing Schwartz, the new ghost "haunting Henry most." Others are very much on his mind in the course of the book—Jarrell, Stevens, Frost, Pound (though still alive), Hemingway—but it is Schwartz whose death reinforces his most nihilistic convictions: "All that is foul smell & blood in a bag." And it is this loss also that most powerfully awakens his own death wish, miserable Henry "who *knew* him all so long, for better & worse / and nearly would follow him below" (156). The intensity of the grief is underscored by the quiet allusion to the marriage vows.

This desire for oblivion, this state of being half in love with easeful death, surfaces again and again, invariably in the context of an undeserved (and unwanted) survival: "All those deaths keep Henry pale and ill / and unable to sail through the autumn world & weak, / a disadvantage of surviving" (191). Maybe it's time "to throw in my own hand" (159) he says early in the section, and later, "There seems to firm no answer / save from the sexton in the place that blinds" (164). He wonders why he alone "breasts the wronging tide," and asserts, "The older you get, at once / the better death looks" (185). It also looks "more fearful & intolerable," however, and while the "desire for death was strong," he defers, at least for the present, following Delmore below.

His preoccupation with dying is closely related to the numerous references to bodily decay. "Three limbs, three seasons smashed; well, one to go" he laments (164), and almost immediately after, "I have strained everything except my ears" (166). In number 198 he lies in a hospital with a broken arm, feeling "real pain between shots from light to light." His system is "nearing an end" (215), he is "completely exhausted" (239), he coughs his "proper blood" (250), his body is "insulted by his life." Henry, in short, "is dying" (199), is in "his final days" (269), or at least feels that he is, and is headed "toward his friendly grave." The images by which he most eloquently describes this sense of his own gradual diminution are related to twilight and fall:

so Henry in twilight is on his own:
marrying, childing, slogging, shelling taxes,
pondering, making.

(201)

The leaves fall, lives fall, every little while
you can count with stirring love on a new loss
& an emptier place.
The style is black jade at all seasons, the style
is burning leaves and a shelving of moss
over each planted face.

(191)

There are also other images by which Henry's obsession is documented. He speaks of Sylvia Plath handing in her credentials,
leaving behind two tots, of Yvor Winters dead of cancer, of a
candle lit for John Kennedy. He refers to the bodies of the self-
drowned, of "shotguns & fathers' suicides," of nuclear devices.
Calamity Jane is pictured in her grave, "her soles to Wild Bill's
skull." "Ashes, ashes, all fall down" sums up his feeling about
inhabiting, still, a deteriorating body in a deteriorating world.

There is, however, another side to Henry, one that nearly bal-
ances his preoccupation with and attraction to death, and this is
that part of him that is unwilling, despite everything, to let go,
that wishes to keep working. Berryman was primarily interested
in people in crisis, and crises always involve the necessity for
choice. "Vanish me later," (196) he says, and "No, I want rest
here, neither below nor above." Again, "Henry has much to do /
Take a deep breath then, sigh, relax, continue." This sense of resignation is something new. It expresses a mellowness, the repeated horror of loss notwithstanding, that is evident in various
quiet ways throughout the section. The autumn of the day, the
fall of the year, and late middle age are traditionally times of
tranquility that precede the chill of night-winter-old age. It is significant that this long sixth book, beginning as it does with a sus-

tained wail of anguish, closes on a note of serenity. Number 274 opens, "It's lovely just here now in the midst of night," and ends with an image of sea-foam tugging "eastward my heart" (to Ireland): "suddenly it all seems quite sane / to a man who has rolled up the rugs." The next song begins "And yet I find myself able, at this deep point, / to carry out my duties: I lecture, I write," and ends "Waiting for fall / and the cold fogs thereof / in delicious Ireland." The three final songs, Henry's farewells, addressed to friends who are moving to California, tell us even more about this changed Henry. He sends hope that their houses will not collapse, asserting "*His* was firm enough." The final song ends with a hopeful image of launching forth, "let's get on toward the sea."

How can we account for these new notes, for these manifestations of sanity and relative peace that help keep the nightmare in check? A possible answer is that his house was indeed firm, that these songs were written during (and recount) a period of domestic stability that served as a buffer against the outside world of deaths and dying. "But the lucid fact of Kate Berryman," William Meredith writes, "during that summer [1962] as during the whole last decade of his life, translated what was difficult about John into terms that less extraordinary people could understand." [19] It is not coincidental that Henry's father is mentioned in only two songs, while his wife and his new daughter are described again and again, always in the most affectionate terms:

> There is a little life upstairs
> playing her nursery rhymes to be considered
> also. And there is a tall life out in the car
> to be considered.
>
> (175)

> . . . O soon we saw that pointy-nose
> was destined to combine

> her blood with Henry's in a little thing.
> If all went well. It all went better, mingling,
> and Little sprang out.
>
> (186)

> I love you.
> Will I forget ever my sole guru
> far in Calcutta. I do not think so.
> Nor will I you.
>
> (192)

> . . . Throng the Fates,
> he couldn't care less, being in love
>
> with his own teeming lady,—whose dorsal fin
> is keeping her nauseous.
>
> (271)

This clearly is not the wife in number 5, written many years earlier, who is a "complete nothing." Jane Howard interviewed Berryman for *Life* during his stay in Ireland, and discovered that he was an outspoken advocate of both marriage and monogamy: "It's terrible to give half your life over to someone else, but it's worse not to." [20] His wife Kate, he added, was the most beautiful woman he had ever seen.

The fires of lust, so evident in the earlier parts, are understandably under control in this section. There is a quiet humor in Henry's paternal hope that his summer students, Mrs. Harris and Mrs. Neevel, "do giant shrimp in olive oil & lemon" for their husbands (254), a far cry from his earlier passion for the young woman filling "her delicious body with chicken paprika." "The lust-quest seems in this case to be over" he says (163), and though he grieves that "He was always in love with the wrong woman" (213), that a "brandished goddess wide-eyed" his nights (214), and that he is "Profoundly troubled over Miss Birnbaum" (227), the final fifty songs in the section document a sense of peace and orderliness in his emotional life.

His other problem, unfortunately, retains its hold on him. Berryman drank, he told Ms. Howard, because, like Henry James, he had the imagination of disaster and hence lived in terror: "We have reason to be afraid. This is a terrible place, but we have to exert our wills. I wake up every morning terrified." [21] References in these songs indicate an attempt—or rather various attempts—to break the dependence on whisky as an easer of the terror, but the efforts always fail. Song 232 comically moves through abstemiousness ("Stand Henry off the sauce") to a decision to jump off the wagon: "the old thrones / topple, dead sober. The decanter, pal!" In number 246, identifying with an old man hunched "blind-sober on his porch," Henry announces "I haven't drunk a drink in 7 days." Several songs later he is advised to give up spirits and steaks. But all such good intentions, we are fully aware by now, are doomed. Henry is a desperately sick man, and by the end of the book he is making a typical request: "a little more whisky please. A little more whisky please." In all of these poems, Lewis Hyde insists, it is not Berryman, or Henry, but alcohol that is talking. [22]

What about Henry's quarrel with his God in this long sixth section? There is a slight easing of the tension, a hint of reconciliation between the battlers, but not before Henry has lashed out vigorously at his archenemy. And it is the Father who is the object of the anger, and not Christ, who is invariably portrayed in a positive light, as in number 234, "The Carpenter's Son," and in such lines as "by the terrible tree / whereon he really hung, for you & me" (200). With the almighty it is a different matter. Though Henry is, on the religious side, "at a loss," he knows that the world appears to be "the act of an aged whore." Moreover, his antagonist is a divine ironist: "God has many other surprises"; "His love must be very strong indeed / considering its products"; "God loves his creatures when he treats them so?" The creator is also deranged, and perhaps "ought to be curbed"; he is "Something disturbed, ill-leased, & with a touch of paranoia." And according to Tambo in his only sustained solo in the section (220), He is black: "My God! they'm be surprised to see Your face."

For all Henry's blasphemous attacks, however, there is a part of him that needs God's paternal discipline—he is like a child who is rebellious but who nevertheless needs the support of his parents. "Dr. God, Push on me. Give it to me harder," he cries, echoing Donne. And the echo reappears in a key song of the section, number 266:

> Dinch me, dark God, having smoked me out.
> Let Henry's ails fail, pennies on his eyes
> never to open more,
> the shires are voting him out of time & place,
> they'll drop his bundle, drunkard & Boy Scout,
> where he was once before:
>
> nowhere, nowhere. Was then the thing all planned?
> I mention what I do not understand.
> I mention for instance Love:
> God loves his creatures when he treats them so?
> Surely one grand *exception* here below
> his presidency of
>
> the widespread galaxies might once be made
> for perishing Henry, whom let not then die.
> He can advance no claim,
> save that he studied thy Word and grew afraid,
> work & fear be the basis for his terrible cry
> not to forget his name.

There is a strong edge of bitterness in this poem, but the final lines suggest nothing so much as "The Collar," George Herbert's portrayal of a man railing against God's injustice until "Me thought I heard one calling, 'child!' / And I reply'd, '*My Lord.*' " The man who studied "thy Word" and grew afraid is the same poet who, in his final book of poems, devotes himself humbly to a celebration of God's plan. By the end of section six he is moving in that direction.

The seventh (and final) book opens with a resolution to "craft better," and whether this is possible "lay in the Hands above," a statement that comes closer even than anything in the preceding book to being a declaration of faith. The prime mover, to be sure, gets the usual Berryman treatment, being referred to as "The Great One" who, like a chairman, hires and fires, as "a careless monster" who takes "the claws with the purr" (Henry often equates God with bears and tigers), and as the record holder for the "worst career." For the most part, however, the bitter antagonism seems to be over, and there is practically no mention at all of the battle. It is significant that Henry's father also virtually disappears in this valedictory book, mellower and more consistently positive than the others. There is one glancing mention of his grave (292), and the section's penultimate poem, purgative and violent, finds Henry engaged in fantasies involving his coffin, but otherwise the suicide that preoccupies Henry in the earlier parts of the sequence is not touched on even in passing.

The unbridled lust, tamed in book six, also all but disappears from the work at this point. "We have beaten down the foulest of them, lust, / and we pace on in peace, like sister & brother," Henry says in a song dedicated to Valerie Trueblood (315). And though he insists on "Massage at all hours," he does so alone, nursing a drink. Whisky still shows up here and there, as do the other by now established themes—guilt, bodily decay, regret, dreams, fame. For the most part, however, the dominant subjects of the earlier sections receive little play. Even Tambo, indispensable earlier as commentator and questioner, appears in only four songs, going out of the poem completely on a typical note of cold comfort: "You got enemies, Mr Bones. I 'low / a-many will seek your skin & your parts below" (374). Henry is by now virtually on his own.

He is, moreover, in a new setting, and this, as much as anything else, accounts for the new tone in these valedictory songs as well as for the book's unusual coherence. It was Benjamin Franklin who said that the best medicine for low spirits is travel. The real subject of the more than one hundred songs is Ireland, and in this old world exhausted Henry takes on a new inflection, his songs an unaccustomed lucidity. The book, the most novelistic of the seven, starts off with a sea journey and then documents in detail Henry's Dublin. Occasionally a song reveals an inner landscape, or even reverts to the States for its detail, but for the most part the work is set under an Irish sky, is drenched in Irish rain, is filled with Irish ghosts—Yeats, Joyce, Synge, Connally, Pearce—and with references to Irish history. By getting away from his routine in Minneapolis, by being forced, as travellers are, to attend to the details of his day by day life in a strange setting, and by being exposed to new voices, new faces, new images, Henry manages, to a large degree, to escape the tyranny of his griefs. The change is clearly good therapy, and though he cannot leave behind his shaming past (even in moments of relative peace he is stabbed by memories) he does manage to elude much that has accounted for his angst.

He takes only five books with him, a Whitman, a *Purgatorio*, a dictionary, an Oxford Bible, and a copy of Yeats's last poems, all works that for years exerted a powerful influence on his mind and art. Yeats was from the beginning the single most important influence on Berryman, and his spirit in particular hovers over the songs. The younger poet had made a pilgrimage to his home some thirty years earlier and now he returns to "have it out" with the Majestic Shade, to discover whether he had read his lesson right. Henry concludes at one point that the Irish poet, obsessed with symbols, "knew nothing about life" (334), and yet as his absorption in ruminations on death increases so too does his attraction to Yeats's transcendental musings. He is especially responsive to a "strangeness in the final notes, never to be resolved" (331). This notion of a creative flowering late in a career is of particular importance to Henry. He sees it in the work of Goya, in "the mysterious final soundings / of Beethoven's 109-10-11 & the Diabelli Variations" (204), and in the last poems of William Carlos Williams, who was not denied the "mysterious late excellence which is the crown / of our trials & our last bride" (324).

Though still relatively young, Berryman had been writing steadily for a great many years, and he obviously sees connections among Yeats's final notes, Williams' late excellence, and his own strange songs, especially since, given his sporadic desire for oblivion, there was an increasing likelihood that these would be among his own final notes—"Surely I've said enough, my mind has been laid open / for thirty years" (209). If he believed, as he apparently did, that a late excellence is the "crown of our trials," then the reception given *Love & Fame,* the book published after the songs, must have been unspeakably bitter. In any case, we find in the seventh book, for the first time, frequent references to his own work (and especially to the present work, now drawing to a close), and to the realization that there is "much to be done, / much to be done" (309). Like any writer whose major effort is nearly completed Berryman (Henry) experiences a sense of freedom, and is willing, for the first time, to think of the sequence as a whole. He takes a lot of ink to Ireland, "having much to say" (280), and early in the section describes himself as an editor-God, picking through his manuscript, "four times too large," to say "who is to lives & who to dies / before my blessed discharge" (281). The liberating end is in sight. In number 293 he speaks of the poem's "ultimate structure," and four songs later describes his craft: "I perfect my metres / until no mosquito can get through." This perception of his own achievement and of the incipient conclusion of his major undertaking accounts, at least in part, for the diminution of the griefs and memories that so torment him earlier in the work.

Memory is still a controlling force, but now the recollections are not so much of recent humiliations as of events that occurred long ago. With the new setting providing perspective on his native land and on his own career, Henry summons forth images from his early life. The "terrors fresh from Henry's shaming past" (326) are, to be sure, still there to be reckoned with, but they are now outflanked by images from the relatively unencumbered years. Henry on ship, for example, remembers his delight at age 21 as he strolled on the topmost deck of another British boat, "high in the windy night, in love with life" (283). He remembers his first visit to Ireland, "the long sweet days of Fall / the long sweet days of youths striving together" (306). Though the years since have been "labor & scrounge" the enduring validity of Henry's youthful joy cannot be denied. He remembers his moments of love, his delight in St. Tropez, Kyoto, his moments with Sonya, and "charming nights when Henry young was moved / by delicate ladies" (373). These spots in time are more significant than "jobs, awards, books." He also remembers his hours in libraries at Columbia, Cambridge, Princeton, and his delight in books he bought (364). Finally, his memories carry him back to South Kent, where as goalie he threw himself out "helter-skelter-whiz" (369). There is a movement here in the direction of *Love & Fame,* in which, having dropped Henry, Berryman gives an uninhibited description of his young manhood, of his conquests and failures. In *The Dream Songs* the mask remains in place, but it is clear that Berryman was more and more preoccupied with the details of his past, with the "long sweet days" that produced this wreck.

He continues, however, to brood, even in calmer moments, on death. Now, increasingly, it is not the loss of others that troubles

Henry's sleep, but his own impending death. He does, indeed, think of those who are gone—he made lists of surviving friends and of those departed, "and took a deep breath." He calls, in his complex investigation of death, for a way to break the topic open "where so many friends have gone." And in a final grieving reference to Delmore Schwartz he says, "That dreadful small-hours hotel death mars all" (344). He still thinks about suicide, but realizes that "the blood & the disgrace," and the "wounds to the survivors" rule this out. He broods, instead, with fear and regret, on natural death, thinking ahead to the event and envisioning his funeral.

In the section's opening song Henry leaves the country of the dead where "he must return & die himself." This helps set the tone for the book. He knows that "the grand sea awaits us, which will then us toss / & endlessly us undo" (303), and asks for more time "to adjust the conflicting evidence, the 'I'm / immortal-&-not' routine" (347). He wonders whether his fine body and useful mind will be forever lost, and comes to realize that when Twissy graduates from Smith he will be gone. His heart sinks at the prospect. He expresses the hopes that he will not be frightened when the time comes, and that nobody will be ashamed of him. Realizing that his efforts "to make himself kill himself" have failed, he hopes for death from a heart attack, during sleep, and imagines the event: "My eyes with which I see so easily / will become closed. My friendly heart will stop" (373). Finally, having accepted his fate he makes a kind of last will and testament, leaving instructions for his funeral, at which a dancer in a short dress, bobbing and dipping, "dances Henry away." Unable to solve the riddle of mortality he can at least plan to commemorate the "terrible gay ocasion" according to his own lights.

Henry's inability to explain the mystery of death or to answer any of the other questions that plague him is something Berryman regarded as serious. "Now Henry is a man with, God

knows, many faults, but among them is not self-understanding,"
he said during his conversation with Richard Kostelanetz. "Henry
is so troubled and bothered by his many problems that he never
actually comes up with solutions, and from that point of view the
poem is a failure." [23] Since the ills that plague Henry—mortality,
bodily decay, a shaming memory, guilt, untamable lust—are
those no one has ever been able to cure, it is odd that Berryman
should be so hard on his persona and, by definition, himself. As
victim and self-analyst, Henry can hardly be expected to pre-
scribe. (Coming up with solutions, moreover, has surely never
been the criterion for successful poetry.) In the same interview
Berryman helps explain why Henry's situation is intrinsically
doomed:

> You ask me why my generation seems so screwed up? . . . It seems
> that they have every right to be disturbed. The current American
> society would drive anybody out of his skull, anybody who is at all
> responsive; it is almost unbearable. . . . From public officials we
> expect to get lies, and we get them in profusion. . . . Perhaps Syl-
> via Plath did the necessary thing by putting her head in the oven,
> having to live with those lies. [24]

This sounds distressingly like interview rhetoric. It does not do
justice to a man whose despair and delight are infinitely more
complex than such generalizations might suggest. Berryman was
not equipped, either by talent or by disposition, to suggest solutions to the problems of civilization, and if Ezra Pound could experience real outrage in the face of something as remote from
himself as interest rates, the sources of Berryman's emotions
were always much more personal, rooted invariably in his own
history. He was a spiritual historian, and his great poem, like
Whitman's, was mainly the outcroppings of his own emotional
and personal nature, "an attempt from first to last, to put *a Person,* a human being [in the second half of the Twentieth Century,

in America] freely, fully, and truly on record." [25] It was not because of the lies of public officials that he was "screwed up," nor were such lies the cause of his death. The shape of a man's life, as of his death, has sources that are more complicated, more mysterious, and it is these, and not the corruption of politicians, that his brave songs explore. Berryman's subject is Henry House, not the White House. His poems, like the man himself, and like the questions that engaged his most serious attention, are not meant to be explained away in bromides. Their purpose, rather, is to terrify and comfort, and this, uneven and baffling as they sometimes are, they do superbly.

CHAPTER 5

After the Songs

> Interviewer: You, along with Lowell, Sylvia Plath,
> and several others have been called a confessional
> poet. How do you react to that label?
> Berryman: With rage and contempt! Next question.

A year or so before his death Berryman told Peter Stitt that until
he was about 35 he never read his reviews, did not, in fact, even
look at them. "I thought it was indifference, but now I'm convinced that I had no skin on—you know, I was afraid of being
killed by some remark. Oversensitivity. But there was an *element*
of indifference in it, and so the public indifference to my work
was countered with a certain amount of genuine indifference on
my part, which has been very helpful since I became a celeb-
rity." [1] He had put on a bit of skin by the time *Love & Fame* was
published in 1970, but was nevertheless depressed by the numerous attacks on the book, attacks that added to the despair
caused by his troubled religious quest and by his addiction. Resentment and self-pity, part of any alcoholic's daily routine, were
given full play.

The response was not altogether unexpected; Berryman realized that the strutting bravado of the first two sections might offend some readers, and that the book as a whole represented a major departure from the much admired dream songs. By the time he had completed the *Songs* he regarded himself as an epic poet, and did not expect to write any more short poems. One day, however, he wrote a line, "I fell in love with a girl," and, liking its factuality, continued in the same vein: "I thought it was as good as any of my early poems . . . moreover it didn't resemble any verse I had written in my entire life, and moreover the subject was entirely new, solely and simply myself. Nothing else . . . I am a scholar in certain fields, but the subject on which I am a real authority is me, so I wiped out all the disguises and went to work. In about five or six weeks I had what was obviously a book called *Love & Fame.*" [2]

Because the work was so unlike his earlier books, Berryman took some prepublication soundings: "Meanwhile, I was in hospital, I was a nervous wreck. I had lost nineteen pounds in five weeks and had been drinking heavily—a quart a day. So I had my publisher . . . xerox a dozen copies, which I sent out to friends . . . looking for reassurance, confirmation, wanting criticism and so on." [3] Richard Wilbur sent a long critique of "Shirley & Auden," and Berryman accepted nearly every suggestion. Others sent letters of reassurance. Edmund Wilson, however, was unimpressed. John Bayley, in an essay in which he likens the book to a late Picasso drawing ("the realized personality of genius implicit in every flick of the pencil"), wonders whether Wilson, who maintained that modern poetry is the prose of Flaubert, Joyce, and Lawrence, had a chance to read it. [4] In fact, Wilson found the book, in spite of striking passages, "hopeless." [5] (That, Berryman said, is like telling a beautiful woman that you like her left small toenail.) And Mark Van Doren's response was apparently most disturbing of all: "He said things like 'original' and 'will be influential,' and 'will be popular,' and so on, but 'will also be feared and hated.' What a surprising letter! It took me days to get used to it, and it took me days even to see what he meant." [6] Later Berryman came to share Van Doren's opinion that the book would indeed be "threatening," not only for its obscenity but also for its grave piety: "You know, the country is full of atheists and they really are going to find themselves threatened by these poems." [7]

It is not very surprising that the book was attacked and misunderstood. The first edition contains something to offend nearly everyone. The unprecedented exhibitionistic revelations of the first two sections, moreover, caused unsympathetic readers to overlook the later poems, which quietly but effectively undercut the hubris of the earlier parts. In the 7,000 lines of the *Songs* Berryman is able to say the most intimate and outrageous things. Since he is speaking through Henry, however, a reader, even if he makes little distinction between poet and persona, can attribute any especially shocking excesses to the imaginary character. It is one thing for Henry Pussycat to lust after every young woman he sees, quite another for John Berryman, sans mask, to announce, in the first stanza of a book, that he fell in love with "a gash" and that he has fathered a bastard. Isn't it, well, *regressive* for a distinguished poet and chair-holding professor to carry on about adolescent fondlings, about student council elections, penis lengths, college grade-point averages, and the number of women (79) he bedded as a young man? Can one take at all seriously a book containing such information?

In his "Scholia" to the second edition (1972) Berryman adopts the same tone that informs his note to *His Toy, His Dream, His Rest,* in which he complains about critics of the *77 Dream Songs* who went so desperately astray. The initial American reception to *Love & Fame,* he says, was "so uncomprehending that I wondered whether I had wasted my time." He gives an analysis of the first poem, and then in a throw-away sentence says "I have killed some of the worst poems in the first edition." Bellow says that Berryman struck out certain poems in the copy he gave him, writing in the margins such words as "Crap!" "Disgusting." [8] Whether the six poems deleted from the second edition are disgusting is a matter of taste, but that they are inferior to the other work in the book is indisputable. One is surprised not that they were deleted but that they were ever included in the first place. Three each are cropped from the second and third sections. "Thank You, Christine" involves a pickup in Cambridge, who says "I'm menstruating, honey: What's the hurry?" The hurry was "a prepotent erection." The young woman, we are told, "did her bloody best," which, given the circumstances, is not one of the noblest lines Berryman ever wrote. "A Letter" and "To B_____ E_____" concern sexual relations with "B," the latter including cunnilingus, e.g., "I sucked your hairs." Dropped from part two are "The Soviet Union," about Stalin, who, though criminal, had "high even heroic qualities," "The Minnesota 8 and the Letter-Writers," about vermin coming "out of the woodwork" to denounce supporters of unpopular causes, and "Regents' Professor Berryman's Crack on Race," of which these lamentable stanzas are representative:

> Let's confront, Blackie! I concur with you,
> we cannot live together in one place
> without—so Jefferson predicted—*war*,
>   and neither of us wants war
>
> or do you? Some to beat off Whitey's balls
> are passionate—we won't put up with that,
> even our nigger-lovers, or, maybe they will!
>   no longer, according to you, after all having any.

There are two minor changes in the second edition. Emery Neff, the villain of "Crisis," who gives young John a "C," becomes merely "Profesor N." And "Mr. [Robert] Creeley," attacked in "In & Out," becomes Mr. C:

> 'Dear Mr. C, A reviewer in *The Times*
> considering 200 poems of yours
> produced over a period of fifteen years
> adjudged them 'crushingly dull': my view too,
>
> though you won't suppose of course I read them all.
> Sir, you are trivial.
> Pray do not write to me again. Pitch defileth.
> Yours faithfully, Henry.'

The deletions affect slightly the overall architecture of the book, which, in its original form, is organized around a series of departures, the first section ending with the poet sailing for England, the second with his saying that were a former mistress to give the word "I'd take the next plane to London," fact and fiction, past and present, delineated by the comparison. With the two final poems dropped, section two now ends "She skipped dinner at Newnham," and the implicit sense of erotic adventure gives an indication of closure which, if somewhat less satisfying than that provided by the London reference, also repeats the sense of a setting forth. The third part ends, in both editions, with Berryman setting out for his wife, the manuscript for the book in his hand, the promiscuous bee of the first section returning "back to the comb," back to "honey Kate."

The question of reinforced and undercut motifs is of particular importance in this book since the poems derive much of their point and all of their irony from a careful patterning of the sequence as a whole. Although Berryman may well have been familiar with Shelly's "An Exhortation," which begins "Chameleons feed on light and air: / Poets' food is love and fame," his title is more likely borrowed from Keats's "When I Have Fears that I

May Cease to Be." At the end of this sonnet, having expressed his fears of not completing his work and of missing out on love, the poet adds, "then on the shore / Of the wide world I stand alone, and think / Till Love and Fame to nothingness do sink." In the second half of Berryman's book this notion of declining to nothingness is fully examined, love and fame, postulated in the first parts as lust and Public Relations, yielding to "husbandship and crafting." The book thus takes a dramatic turn at the beginning of section three, progressing from the poet's randy and confident young manhood to his depressed present, from ribald skirt-chasing and self-promotion to a humble series of prayers to God, who judges a man's merit not by his verses but by his virtue. Berryman, in his Scholia, says that each of the four movements (he means, I think, each of the last three) criticizes backward the preceding one, but the book can more helpfully be analyzed in terms of its two halves, the second representing a repudiation of the values inherent in the two sections that make up the first.

There is some foreshadowing of this dramatic shift in the opening poems, exuberant and racy as they are. Part one, set in Columbia, traces the poet's career from incoming freshman to budding poet off to the Old World. Berryman takes his cue from a later Columbia man, Allen Ginsberg, whose aim was "tell it all. Poets! . . Lovers & secrets!" The protagonist has already achieved, if not fame, a certain local notoriety:

> I wore white buckskin shoes with tails sometimes
> & was widely known on Morningside Heights,
>
> a tireless & inventive dancing man.

The poems, bristling with high spirits and confidence, document this dancing man's education in the world of the flesh, his tutors being Garnette, Louise, Shirley C., and several other young women. His fantasy at twenty is to satisfy all of Barnard & Smith "& have enough left over for Miss Gibbs's girls." And all of this, of course, is well before the days of coeducational dormitories and the pill. (One gets no inkling from this book, by the way, that Berryman attended college from 1932 to 1936. The only depression he mentions is his own: "I wondered every day about suicide.")

He also discovers the life of the mind, gaining heroes (Auden, Yeats, Pound, Eliot, Joyce, Hume, Blackmur, Unamuno), scapegoats (Ruskin, Carlyle, Emery Neff), and a calling (to create "big fat fresh original & characteristic poems"). Thinking often of his father, "boxed in & let down," he finds a surrogate parent in Mark Van Doren, who welcomes him, following "five monk's months" penance (for academic sloth), as "the Prodigal Son." When not trying to get girls to bed he seeks fame of various sorts, as a politician, poet, editor, "Phi Bete," and dancing man. Like all young men he experiences moments of despondency, but for the most part the Columbia years are characterized by robust energy and unclouded hopes.

Where, then, are the suggestions of the fall from grace to come? They are found in several poems in which the shadow of the present falls on the sunny reminiscences of tumescent young manhood, in which one catches glimpses of a Henry (if I may) who doesn't do much dancing any more. At the end of "Shirley & Auden," for example, the poet addresses "Lithest Shirley":

> But darling, sister, do you yourself ever dance any more?
> My heart quails as I put this unbearable question,—
> into what faraway air?

It is because the answer is so certain that the question is unbearable. There is also a reference in this poem to Auden's "facile bodiless later books," and these works, along with the suggestion of Shirley's danceless state, serve as intimations of the poet's parallel decline. It is also significant that he now calls "sister" this woman who years ago aroused his sexual passion. "Teach me / to see them as sisters & daughters," he prays in part four, asking to be guarded against "impulse lust."

The book's first poem, "Her & It," also contrasts past and present. The poet mentions a girl he once loved who now probably has "seven lousy children," and, after boasting that Saul and he have been praised by *Time* (a quintessential form of American fame), concludes "She muttered something in my ear I've forgotten as we danced." These forgotten words are like the lost photographs ("wishing I could lay my old hands somewhere on those snapshots") in "Images of Elspeth." "In & Out" introduces Al Barabas, who scored a touchdown at the Rose Bowl, and who now writes asking Berryman for a contribution to the College. The request leads into two stanzas that bring the nightmare present into the hopeful world of these poems: the poet sends money instead to found a prize in the name of a suicide, met in hospital, who pounded a punching bag until her knuckles bled, cursing "John Berryman! . . . John Berryman!" So much for the glories of the Rose Bowl. And the excessively vindictive dismissal of Robert Creeley at the end of the poem, moving as far as possible from the "verve I flooded toward in *Don Giovanni*," serves to presage the vistas of what must be endured, "cold girls, fear, thoughtless books."

Berryman, perhaps unconsciously, also introduces other contrasts in the section which, while not explicitly reinforcing the fall from past delight to present dejection, play ironic variations on the theme of fact and illusion. During his studies with Van Doren, for example, the young poet does an intensive analysis of John Locke's *Essay*, but when he gets out into the real world (assuming that Canada so qualifies) he finds himself attracted to "Dr. Locke," who "cured any and everything with foot 'adjustments.' " This speaks volumes for the state of the young graduate who, as he says, "felt dazed." The statement of the young friend who mutters in "Freshman Blues" that "his penis was too small" is varied in "Two Organs" by the elderly scholar who, urinating from a boat, exclaims "I wish my penis was big enough for this whole lake!" (Even though the crucial word here is "wish," this is the only moment in the book in which the present is shown to an advantage.) Finally, the picture of the youthful Berryman as dancing man gives way to the image of his friend in Canada, "in a wheel-chair," which in turn looks toward the image of the poet, at the end of part three, leaving the hospital "lurching on my left toe," the tireless dancing man brought nearly to a halt.

Since part one ends with the poet on board the *Britannic* vowing to visit by hook or crook with Yeats it is surprising that the Irish poet scarcely appears in part two, though the fact that the visit is documented in one of the dream songs may account for its absence here. There is also no mention of Dylan Thomas in any of the second section's ten poems. Instead we have novelistic descriptions of a young man experiencing euphoria during the boat trip, settling into Cambridge, exploring the city's history and bookstores, feeling alienated and lonely during months of unwilling monkhood, and finally meeting and bedding "the most passionate & versatile actress in Cambridge." The poems that precede this conquest are mostly bookish, filled with the sort of Cambridge-based guidebook details that stocked the eager young scholar's mind. Except for the exhilaration of the shipboard lyrics, accounted for by the presence on the *Britannic* of Pedro Donga, and of the last poems, involving the young woman, the work is less exhuberant than that of the first section. On a few occasions, moreover, as in the Columbia poems, the presence of the older Berryman tends to cast a chill over the generally pleasant reminiscences. In "Views of Myself," for example, assuming the role of Coriolanus, he makes this painful confession:

> When I was fiddling later with every wife
> on the Eastern seaboard
> I longed to climb into a pulpit & confess.
> Tear me to pieces!

Another detail from the years ahead involves the President of his
Form at South Kent who "killed himself, I never heard why / or
just how, it was something to do with a bridge."

The mood of the section, quietly academic, is well characterized by "The Other Cambridge," of which these stanzas are representative:

> Mother of Newton & Wordsworth! Milton & lazy Gray;
> imperious Bentley, Porson wittier than Byron,
> 'Yes, Mr Southey is indeed a wonderful poet.
> He will be read when Homer & Virgil are forgotten.'
>
> (Byron always spoiled it by adding 'But not till then.')
> Drunks for six centuries while the towers flew
> skyward & tranquil punts poled under tranquil bridges:
> David's forever new bookstall in Market Hill
>
> where for shillings I bought folios
> of Abraham Cowley of O delectable 'The Chronicle':
> the 1594 Prayer Book by twelve Cambridge men
> & one outlander: Peterhouse' formal garden. . . .

There is a nice air of delight and discovery in this bristling punctuation and name-dropping, a sense of participating in a brave
new world that would become even richer with the erotic relationship that concludes the section.

With part three, however, we leave behind all the discoveries
and pretensions, the hubris and awkwardness, the hope and energy. The poet now focuses exclusively on the present, and it is
very grim indeed, any illusions of love and fame, as they exist in
the earlier parts, disappearing completely. In spite of the four-

line stanza, in fact, much of this section, brooding and death-obsessed, resembles the darker music of the *Songs:*

> *Losses!* as Randall observed
> who walked into a speeding car
> under a culvert at night in Carolina
> having just called his wife to make plans for the children.
> "Relations"

> I am busy tired mad lonely & old.
> O this has been a long long night of wrest.
> "Damned"

> Reflexions on suicide, & on my father, possess me.
> I drink too much. My wife threatens separation.
> She won't 'nurse' me. She feels 'inadequate'.
> We don't mix together.
> "Of Suicide"

> It seems to be DARK all the time
> I have difficulty walking.
> I can remember what to say to my seminar
> but I don't know that I want to.
> I said in a Song once: I am unusually tired.
> I repeat that & increase it.
> I'm vomiting.
> I broke down today in the slow movement of K. 365.
> "Despair"

These excerpts appear to be pretty much of a piece. In fact, however, the section, the richest and most moving of the four, has considerable thematic range, far more than any other. It is constructed as a descent into the dark night of the soul that is followed by a gradual recovery, or, to use a word that figures importantly in two of the later poems, by *survival.*

Its first poem, "The Search," opens with the recounting of a dream in which both the poet and his works die, thus collapsing any hope for "women & after-fame." The unnerving dream is fol-

lowed by a description of the poet's search for spiritual understanding, in which Keats, Blake, Vaughan, and Wordsworth are
replaced by the Biblical exegesists Guignebert, Bultmann, Wel-
lisch, Luther. "Message," which follows, sums up such wisdom as
the poet has been able to evolve: "Children! Children! form the
point of all. / Children & high art." These themes are repeated in
"Relations," in the mention of Jarrell's making plans for the children, and in references to Elizabeth Bishop, Emily Dickinson,
and Marianne Moore. (This poem is probably Berryman's penance for Song 187, in which Henry announces "Them lady poets
must not marry, pal.") "Antitheses" then wittily documents the
two sorts of creators of "high art," the vague (such as Auden,
whose socks didn't match) and the hard-headed, like Victor
Hugo. The next poem, "Have a Genuine American Horror-&-
Mist on the Rocks," about nerve-gas rockets transported through
the South, seems to be out of place in this section. A case can be
made for it, however, because it documents a sick civilization
("the 20th Century flies insanely on"), and Berryman, as well as
the others introduced in the later poems, are products and manifestations of this madness. In the next poem the poet advises a
woman (the implications are that he is addressing all women) to
escape this sickness by asserting her independence. This is followed by the poem ending "Man is a huddle of need." Then
"Damned," foreshadowing a Dantesque sequence, describes, in
remarkably explicit terms, an adulterous affair ("I was scared &
guilty"), one result of which, apparently, is the illegitimate child
referred to in the book's first poem: "(I've three myself, one
being off the record.)" The difference in tone between this poem
and those describing his Columbia and Cambridge conquests
could hardly be greater.

Following other work that further develops the themes of
madness and paternity we encounter a five-poem cluster, set "in
hospital" (as Berryman, with his British locutions, always put it),

which documents a Dantesque progression: "The Hell Poem,"
"Death Ballad," and " 'I Know' " lead to "Purgatory," followed,
in turn, by "Heaven." "Hell" is divided into two circles, the one
in which the poet and a group of women suffer "anguishes, gnaw-
ings," the other placed behind a locked door, "back there,"
where the worst victims are kept. The horror of the life "back
there" is matched by the fear of the outside, the now desired but
frightful world beyond the hospital. In this hell the poet has a
dream about a headless child, which relates not only to his illegitimate son but also to his serious doubts about his work—in "Two
Organs" he describes his "uterine struggles" to give birth to original and characteristic poems.

"Death Ballad," focusing on the sucide pact of "Tyson & Jo," is
important because it takes the poet outside his own despair and
evokes his compassion for other suffering souls. In the last stanza
he counsels the doomed girls:

> take up, outside your blocked selves, some small thing
> that is moving
> & wants to keep on moving
> & needs therefore, Tyson, Jo, your loving.

One is reminded of Eliot's notion of some infinitely gentle, infinitely suffering thing. The stanza also suggests that moment in
which Coleridge's Ancient Mariner blesses the sea creatures and
is thus able to begin his journey home. Berryman is doing what
he advises the girls to do: he has found outside his own blocked
self two troubled individuals, Tyson and Jo, who need, and receive, his love. This unselfconscious giving, continued in the next
poem in his concern for Hilary, Laana, and Jeff (who "paws my
right arm, & cries"), is largely responsible for his ascent out of
the depths of anguish.

"Purgatory," a leave-taking poem, comments on those fellow
inmates the poet will miss after he departs. His main tribute is

reserved for the dining room manager, Mrs. Massey, who has managed somehow to survive. She is a source of hope: "And if *you* can carry on so, so maybe can I." There is one person the poet will not miss, a black woman who has told the group that she will kill herself between the ages of 62 and 67: "Arrogant, touchy, vain, self-pitying, & insolent: / I haven't been spoken to so for thirteen years." There is a nice irony in Berryman's violent response to this woman whose "outrageous" behavior is, after all, a mirror image of his own throughout much of his life. His own outrage is unintentionally comic.

The themes of survival and loss reappear in the last of the poems in the Dante sequence, "Heaven," which traces the transition from lust to love. Against a backdrop of cathedrals in Seville and Venice the poet reminisces about a woman with whom years ago he spent an Easter afternoon and who was later killed in an accident. His passion has changed to the mourning of a survivor, and to prayers to the spirits of night, who "Sing on with her." The lyric sets the stage for "The Home Ballad," which finds the speaker "severely damaged, but functioning." In this final poem of the section the rescued Mariner, hobbling on one foot, carries his typescript book, containing his "almost hopeless angry art," home to "honey Kate." We must "work & play," he announces at the poem's opening, and at the end he makes a hopeful but doomed resolution that is, more than anything else, a conscientious effort to keep up his courage: "Tomorrow we'll do our best, our best, / tomorrow we'll do our best." Even though we suspect that this state of relative calm is destined to be temporary, the poem, with its references to freedom, to home, and to his wife, represents, after the despair of the hospital sequence, a decisive breakthrough.

In the "Eleven Addresses to the Lord" that make up part four, a self-effacing and reverent suppliant completes his separation from the sort of love and fame introduced in the New York and Cambridge poems. "Guard me / against my flicker of impulse lust," he prays, and in another prayer, quoting Hopkins, asserts that "the only true literary critic is Christ." [9] Berryman by now is willing to be God's scrivener. "At Thy dictation / I sweat out my wayward works," he announces, and throughout the poems God is addressed as a superior fellow artist: "craftsman," "Inimitable contriver," "master of insight," a "delicious author." The poet regards himself, by contrast, as an apprentice, an imitator whose most careful work is dismissed as a "thing." And in the last poem he is a mere student who, if worthy, as were Germanicus and Polycarp, will receive his degree, "which then thou wilt award." He wishes to be ready with his witness, a far cry from the young man who, like Jacob with his father's blessing, "set forth to con the world."

In these prayers, as in the hospital poems, Berryman is able to get outside his own tormented skin, able to express his concern for others: for the lost souls in ill-attended wards, for his children ("Postpone till after my children's deaths your doom"), his wife ("strengthen my widow"), "desolate Sherry," his friends ("Ease in their passing my beloved friends"), and "my mother far & ill." For himself he asks a blessing gratuitous, and, in a passage reminiscent of Herbert's "The Pulley," for rest: "Rest may be your ultimate gift." He is also asking, in a more implicit fashion, for faith, and this is the main burden of these respectful but speculative addresses. "I believe," he seems to be saying, "help thou my unbelief."

I say speculative because in the first five prayers Berryman is recording, more than anything else, his confusion. He can feel awe but not love for what is essentially unknowable, and having no idea "whether we live again" he awaits enlightenment. God's ways are incomprehensible, involving "buds sticky in Spring," but also Belsen and Omaha Beach.

> Across the ages certain blessings swarm,
> horrors accumulate, the best men fail:

> Socrates, Lincoln, Christ mysterious.
> Who can search Thee out?

The sixth prayer, however, represents a turning point, speculation suddenly giving way to belief. "Under new management, Your Majesty: / Thine." For the first time since his father's suicide blew out his faith and left him spiritually bankrupt he has had his eyes opened. He is, in fact, even able to indicate the precise moment of his revelation: "My double nature fused in that point of time / three weeks ago day before yesterday." The awkwardness of the phrasing does not detract from the importance of the event. By the eighth prayer he is able to state unequivocally, "I do not understand, but I believe," and in the penultimate prayer, "I fell back in love with you, Father," a nice variation on the book's opening: "I fell in love with a girl." (Given, moreover, that he lost his father and his God at the same moment, some forty odd years earlier, his epithet is apt.) In his *Paris Review* interview he was asked why he began to write religious poems, and responded: "They are the result of a religious conversion which took place on my second Tuesday in treatment here last spring. [The interview took place in late October 1970 in the extended-care ward at St. Mary's Hospital, the setting of the poems in section three and for *Recovery*.] I lost my faith several years ago, but I came back—by force, by necessity, because of a rescue action—into the notion of a God who, at certain moments, definitely and personally intervenes in individual lives, one of which is mine. The poems grew out of that sense, which not all Christians share." [10]

The rescue that precipitated the conversion is a matter of considerable importance. During the campus unrest brought on by Cambodia and Kent State the poet, feeling that his students needed calming, was to taxi from the hospital to lecture on the fourth Gospel. On the morning of the class his permission was rescinded and, though shocked and defiant, he finally submitted after his fellow patients failed to support him. It was while he was in a state of despair that his counselor, an Episcopal priest, "rescued" him by offering to give the lecture.

> Well when I thought it over in the afternoon, I suddenly recalled what has been for many years one of my favorite conceptions. I got it from Augustine and Pascal. It's found in many other people too, but especially in those heroes of mine. Namely, the idea of a God of rescue. He saves men from their situations, off and on during life's pilgrimage, and in the end. I completely bought it, and that's been my position since . . . [After losing my faith at twelve] I never lost the sense of God in the two roles of creator and sustainer—of the mind of man and all its operations, as a source of inspiration to great scientists, great artists, great statesmen. But my experience last spring gave me a third sense, a sense of a God of rescue, and I've been operating with that sense.[11]

One of the "heroes of mine" Berryman might have mentioned is Crane, whose story "The Monster" he praises in his critical study. It concerns a Negro named Henry Johnson who is hostler to a doctor. Henry rescues the doctor's boy from a fire, and in so doing has his face destroyed by acid and his mind unhinged, surviving as a "monster" with no face. Berryman sees Oedipal elements in Crane's identification with "veiled and shamed" Henry, in the writer's rivalry against the father, the wish to be the father. In his own prayer, however, Berryman becomes the submissive child, the good son, in no way competing with or fighting the rescue by the Father with whom he has fallen back in love. He identifies with everyone, "even the heresiarchs," and is eager for God's blessing.

If this somewhat pedantic final section of *Love & Fame* is pervaded by the spirits of Father Hopkins, Justin Martyr, Augustin, and Polycarp, the work as a whole pays tribute to another of Berryman's idols. In "Dante's Tomb" we find these lines:

> . . . Hundreds & hundreds of little poems
> rolled up & tied with ribbons
> over the virgin years, 'unwanted love'.

Love and fame in the conventional American sense were as unknown to Emily Dickinson as they were to Hopkins, and it says
something about the nature of Berryman's quest that he selects
her four-line stanza as his form. In so doing he brings her into the
present, not, as with Anne Bradstreet, to seduce her spirit, but to
enlist her aid in an attempt to get as many things as possible absolutely correct. "Writing," he said, "is just a man alone in a
room with the English language trying to make it come out right.
The important thing is that your work is something no one else
could do." [12]

The poems were written in a burst of energy during a five- or
six-week period, and this helps account for their stylistic unifor-
mity. The stanza, unrhymed, with four lines of varying length
(anywhere from four to twenty-one syllables), sometimes falling
into regular pentameter, is the norm upon which all variations
are played. Half of the book's poems adhere to the stanza, the
prayers being the most regular, with no deviations at all. What
changes there are invariably involve the addition of a fifth line,
for emphasis. In ten poems the added line stands alone as a final
stanza. This one-line conclusion, with its abrupt assertion, serves,
like the couplet in some Shakespearean sonnets, to tie together
the details of the preceding stanzas, e.g., "wishing I could lay my
old hands somewhere on those snapshots" ("Images of Elspeth");
"She skipped dinner at Newnham" ("Tea"); "Utter, His Father,
one word" ("Despair"). The last quoted phrase is unusual in that
there is no punctuation to provide final closure. Eighty percent of
the stanzas are end-stopped, and the percentage increases from
the first half of the book to the second—as the poet moves toward
the present the units become more and more closed, self-con-

tained, the statements more terse. There are only eight run-on stanzas in the second half of the book. Seventy-seven percent of the stanzas in the first half are end-stopped, and ninety-five percent in the second half, or breaking the figure down further: seventy percent in part one, seventy-four percent in two, ninety-three percent in three, and one hundred percent in four.

There is no regular rhythmical pattern from poem to poem, from stanza to stanza, or even from line to line, though at times Berryman has taken pains to give the lines a regular iambic pattern, as these representative examples indicate:

> I wísh she'd réad my bóok & wríte to mé
> from Ó wheréver áh how fár she ís
>
> .   .   .
>
> I díd not cénsor ánythíng I sáid
> & whát I sáid I sáid with fórce & wít
>
> .   .   .
>
> I sérved at Máss six dáwns a wéek from fíve,
> adóring Fáther Bóniface & yóu,
> mémorízing the Látin hé expláined.
> Móstly we wórked alóne. Óne or twó wómen.

The shift in the last quotation from the regular second line to the jagged and conversational third and fourth is a favorite Berryman technique, one that permits him to use the blank verse that comes so naturally (especially after decades of use) and at the same time to maintain the clipped, idiomatic rhythms of this essentially conversational book. On occasion the regular and the seemingly irregular alternate:

> I mét a cóp who cálled him Dón Miguél;
> anóther of my sóphomore héroes.
> And Dávid Húme stood hígh with mé that yéar
> & Kléist, for the 'Púppet-théatre'.

This is actually quite elegant, the five and three stress lines alternating (like Dickinson's four and three stress lines), but with the second and fourth breaking the pentameter just enough to give the illusion of raggedness, an impression that disappears if the lines are read aloud two or three times.

Many of the poems, particularly in the first two parts, are prosy and free. One generally gets the sense of a voice talking naturally, informally, without embellishment, the phrases produced by the breath and by the details that make up the telling rather than by adherence to a rhythmical norm. Compare the following two passages:

> He sings me a Basque folk-song, his father was Basque, passing through, his mother a Spanish lady married, staying there. He ran away at nine, with gypsies. At the University of Lyon he assisted with experiments in resuscitation, he says the Russians are ahead of us in this field. He sang then for a night-club in Berlin & got 50 sexual offers a week. With Memel, the Belgian composer he went to the Congo to collect tribal tunes.

> .   .   .

> It was not Death for I stood up and all the Dead lie down. It was not Night, for all the Bells put out their Tongues, for noon. It was not Frost, for on my Flesh I felt—siroccos—crawl—Nor Fire—for just my Marble feet Could keep a Chancel, Cool—

There is no question about the line endings in the Dickinson poem, but even the most gifted reader would find it nearly impossible to identify the breaks in a large percentage of the Berryman lines if they were printed like the passage above from "First Night at Sea."

There are a few poems in the book that have fairly conventional rhythmical patterns—that is, they can be scanned—and these contrast dramatically with the work's more representative idiomatic passages. Some of the more regular poems are deceptive, seeming at first to strive for a singsong regularity that doesn't quite fall into place, that sounds, in fact, more chaotic than harmonious. If the lines are read aloud several times, however, one begins to hear underlying rhythms which, anything but clumsy, are hauntingly beautiful. I choose a stanza from "The Home Ballad" as an example.

> Īt's hóme tŏ mȳ dáughtēr Ī cóme ‖
> wīth vérsēs & stóriēs trúe, ‖
> whīch Ī cōuld ālsō shāre wīth yŏu,
> mȳ déar, mȳ déar, ‖
> ōnlȳ yōu aɾe nŏt mȳ dáughtēr.

The literary ballad meter of the first two lines, each of which is followed by a strong caesura, gives way to the folk ballad meter (or talking ballad) of the next three. An effective reading requires an unusually strong stress on "you," at the end of line three, a long pause at the end of line four, and strong emphasis on "not" and "daught" in the last line, the internal rhyme providing closure.

A similar strategy can be discovered in the final stanza of the poem:

> Īt's *Lóve & Fáme* cālled, ‖hónēy Káte, ‖
> yōu réad īt fróm thē stárt ‖
> ánd ‖sómetímes ‖Ī réel ‖whēn yōu práise mȳ árt ‖
> mȳ hónēy ‖ālmōst hópelēss ‖ángrȳ ‖árt, ‖
> whīch wās bóth oūr Fáte—

Again, the literary ballad meter modulates into that of the folk ballad, and in the final three lines the frequent strong caesurae add immeasurably to the overall effect, as does an especially heavy stress on "reel." It helps if one is able to imagine a pub singer projecting these lines with rushed syllables and long pauses where the music fills in the rhythm.

In contrast to these evocative stanzas there are passages here and there in the book that are technically weak. These lapses are anything but unobtrusive, and yet they do not really account for the fact that *Love & Fame* has been almost universally reviled, regarded more often than not as a sequence of poetic mistakes that should never have been published. There are, I believe, two principal reasons for this low critical esteem. The work, first of all, unlike *Mistress Bradstreet* and *The Dream Songs*, is not a good seminar text, and a generation of teachers and critics responsive to the labyrinths of Nabokov, Robbe-Grillet, Pynchon, Lowell, Beckett, and others (including Berryman himself) find little here to unravel or to illuminate. There are so few mysteries, metaphysical and stylistic (the most engaging problems, as I have suggested, are structural) that the most one can do by way of explication in many cases is simply read a poem out loud. What is one to demonstrate, after all, about lines, however crafty, that sound so much like unembellished prose? Finding themselves with virtually nothing to say, critics have assumed that it is the poems themselves that lack inspiration.

The book has also been consistently misread, or worse, not read at all, by those who damn it most vigorously. If one believes, with Louis Simpson, that the poets who followed Eliot, Williams, and Pound, the generation of Lowell, Berryman, Schwartz, and others, "had only a desperate, insatiable desire for fame,"[13] then a book called *Love & Fame*, filled with name-dropping, preening, and references to the author's media triumphs, is clearly going to be a red flag. And if a reader is so annoyed by the poet's supposed vanity that he fails to notice that love and fame finally sink to nothingness, then the capacity for misinterpretation is virtually limitless. An example (unfortunately not isolated) of an inattentiveness to the text that borders on the bizarre is found in *The Confessional Poets* by Robert Phillips.[14] The thesis of a brief, unpleasant chapter called "John Berryman's

Literary Offenses" (if indeed a series of snide jokes and wrong-headed observations can be said to have a thesis) is that the poet was interested in nothing but lust and money, and that his poems are blatantly self-promoting. Berryman, Phillips writes, "clearly came to equate fame with money. The book also demonstrates that for him love had become equated with lust. It is this self-aggrandizement and lack of compassion which make Berryman's late confessions a series of false notes. . . . Rather than display-ing moral courage, these poems display instead immoral callow-ness. In place of love and fame, we have lust and notoriety." [15] Apparently agitated by the alleged offenses of the first parts, this critic has not bothered to read carefully the absolutely crucial third section—at one point, in fact, he announces that the "for-midable ego which wrote the poems of the first three sections has never been sufficiently doubtful or suffered the mental disquie-tude which would trigger such a full-scale embracing of Chris-tianity" as is seen in the final section. [16] Obviously those whose evaluations are based on prejudice rather than on perception are going to find much to despise in this unconventional book. Ber-ryman, however, like Joyce, Pound, and others who have been subjected to inane misinterpretation, is too powerful a writer to be harmed, ultimately, by this sort of sniping.

In defending this book against its more extreme detractors I certainly do not mean to imply that it represents the crowning glory of Berryman's prolific career. William Heyen, taking a posi-tion as different as possible from that of Phillips, asserts that Ber-ryman is the only genius he has ever met, then adds "it is my feeling that he came to this Genius at the end of his life in *Love & Fame* (1970) and *Delusions, Etc.* (1972), that we will find this out, and that this will take a long time." [17] As I make clear in my next chapter, I regard *Love & Fame* as a finer book, by a good deal, than *Delusions, Etc.* It is not, however, either so brilliant or so startlingly eccentric as *Mistress Bradstreet* or *The Dream*

Songs. There is, nevertheless, after the intricacies of these two superb sequences, much that can be said for a work that strives for direct, unambiguous communication, and that more often than not achieves its goal. Lacking this vulnerable book, whatever its shortcomings, the Berryman canon would be noticeably slighter.

CHAPTER 6

Islands of Suffering: The Last Books

Unfazed, you built-in the improbable.
You clowned. You made throats swallow
and shivered the backs of necks.
You made quiver with glee, at will; not long.
The world is of male energy male pain.
                                    "Beethoven Triumphant"

A volume called *Henry's Fate and Other Poems*, published in Spring 1977, is the fourth Berryman book published by Farrar, Straus & Giroux since the poet's death in 1972. *Delusions, Etc.,* the final collection of poems, came out in 1973, *Recovery* in 1974, and *The Freedom of the Poet,* the rich harvest of previously un-collected critical essays, in 1976. (In a superb review of the latter book, Donald Davie expresses his view that "the man behind this book was not only one of the most gifted and intelligent Americans of his time, but also one of the most honorable and responsible.") [1] Given the quantity of material in the University of Minnesota archives—stories, letters, journals, etc.—we can almost certainly look for still more books to appear over the years.

The work in *Henry's Fate,* which consists of forty-five un-

collected or unpublished dream songs (some of which are marvelous), twenty-one lyrics of varying length, and four fragments, is
drawn from the last six years of the poet's life. This period
(1967–1972) saw the publication of both *His Toy, His Dream, His
Rest* and *Love & Fame*, and nearly all of the *Henry's Fate* poems
show important connections, technical and thematic, with the
work of these earlier volumes, many of the poems clearly being
either offshoots or rejects. The poems in *Delusions, Etc.*, already
in proof at the time of Berryman's death, were all composed during his final months, and as such this volume represents the real
culmination of the poetic journey that took him from the re-
strained elegance of the early lyrics through the mannered confessions of the sonnets, to the compressed intensity of *Anne Bradstreet*, the eccentric drama of the dream songs, the lucid
revelations of *Love & Fame*, and finally to these nervous, obscure
religious musings.

The "Etc." of the title is deceptive, a casual gesture that
suggests an informality that is utterly at odds with the puzzlingly
dense character of the book. And what, after all, does "et cetera"
encompass—fears? suspicions? guilt? renunciations? We never
quite find out, for the title serves as an earnest of other obscuri-
ties to follow. What we do know is that like the latter *Songs* and
like *Love & Fame*, this "final" book has as its central concerns
questions of belief and doubt, reinforcing the view that the later
Berryman is a religious poet par excellence, a man engaged in a
strenuous, nearly obsessive dialogue with his God. Of the forty-
three poems in the book, twenty-six have explicitly theological
themes, and several others also give evidence of the poet's troubled sense of being dispossessed, and of his preoccupation with
questions of grace. (The sense of spiritual well-being that permeates the last pages of *Love & Fame* was, unfortunately, short-
lived.) At times nearly unbearable in their tortured intensity,
many of the poems resemble the darkest of Hopkins' sonnets.

The book is divided into five sections, the first and last bearing directly on the poet's relationship with his God. Part one, "Opus Dei," opens with an epigraph on which variations are played throughout the book: "And he did evil, because he prepared not his heart to seek the Lord." This opening sequence of eleven poems is structured around the canonical hours, not, the poet tells us, through one day, but over many weeks. They reveal the poet at his prayers, at "Lauds," "Matins," "Prime," "Tierce," "Sext," "Nones," "Vespers," and "Compline." (An "Interstitial Office" is placed between "Prime" and "Tierce.") These lyrics are expressions of fear, shame, and suspicion. They communicate the poet's ambivalent yearnings in a language that is clotted and obscure, one that lacks completely the vernacular ingeniousness of *Love & Fame.* The transition from book to book could hardly be greater:

> Lo, where in this whirlpool sheltered in bone,
> only less whirlpool bone, envisaging,
> a sixtieth of an ounce to every pint,
> sugar to blood, or coma or convulsion . . .

The book's final section also consists of eleven poems, again all centered on the poet's relationship with his God, as indicated by such titles as "Somber Prayer," "A Usual Prayer," "The Prayer of the Middle-Aged Man." This series resembles canonical hours without any sequential pattern. The last two poems bring the section, and the book, to a rousing conclusion. In "The Facts & Issues" the poet experiences a profound sense of God's presence, but expresses, nevertheless, a feeling of intense self-loathing, concluding on a note of despair that is suicidal:

Let me be clear about this. It is plain to me
Christ underwent man & treachery & socks
& lashes, thirst, exhaustion, the bit, for *my* pathetic & disgusting vices,

to make this filthy fact of particular, long-after,
faraway, five-foot-ten & moribund
human being happy. Well, he has!
I am so happy I could scream!
It's *enough!* I can't BEAR ANY MORE.
Let this be it. I've *had* it. I can't wait.

One hardly expects Berryman to supplant the mood induced by
these diminishing climaxes. The book ends, however, on a positive note, its concluding poem showing King David, surrounded
by hypocrites and a shallow wife, vigorously asserting his existence: "all the black same I dance my blue head off!" Even
though "King David Dances" is, except for this final line, rather
flat, the poem provides the collection with an affirmative and,
given the circumstances of Berryman's death, disturbing conclusion.

The three sections that stand between the opening and closing
religious sequences are diverse and altogether odd. The second
section celebrates five admirable "makers," beginning with
George Washington and ending with Dylan Thomas. These artists comprise a nearly unbroken chronological chain that links
three centuries. Washington lived from 1732 to 1799, Beethoven,
the subject of the second poem, from 1770 to 1827, and Emily
Dickinson from 1830 to 1886. George Trakl was born the year
after Dickinson's death, and died in 1914, the year Dylan
Thomas, the fifth subject, was born, as was Berryman himself.
The poems, none of which is concerned with the quest for God
(though as one of the epigraphs maintains, "L'art est réligieux"),
are for the most part bookish and often obscure, drawing many of
their details from the poet's reading.

Part three, even more obscure and overall quite poor, is a mis-
cellany, the poems of which have little apparent relation to one
another or, often, to the work as a whole. The section does, however, contain "He Resigns," in its eloquent understatement as
moving as anything Berryman wrote:

> I don't want any thing
> or person, familiar or strange.
> I don't think I will sing
>
> any more just now;
> or ever. I must start
> to sit with a blind brow
> above an empty heart.

The quiet anguish in these uncluttered lines makes them considerably more affecting than the more agitated assertions in such poems as "Back":

> Exceptional, singular, & mysterious,
> ochered, forbidden to utter,
> the revolted novice & veteran thro' cold night
> vigilant in the forest, a caring beast,
>
> becoming sacral, perforates his nose
> at first glow . . .

Many lyrics in this section, as in the book as a whole, are extraordinarily private, far more so than anything in the more obviously confessional dream songs.

The fourth section, labelled "Scherzo," provides a slightly animated movement just preceding the measured dance of the finale. Three of its five poems are outright failures, one a petulant request to God to let the poet's critics "have it," another about James Dickey, its source the poet's happiness "to see a good guy *get out* of the advertising racket." The two that succeed are dream songs, explicitly about Henry, and coming upon them is like unexpectedly encountering old friends at a party full of high-strung noisy strangers. More accessible than most of the songs, they provide two unsettling views of a nocturnal Henry. In the first he is shown suffering a bout of insomnia, rambling around the house and generally destroying any peace his wife might seek in sleep. In the second, which is exceptionally moving, he remembers a visit some twenty-five years ago to a friend's place in Maine where he experienced a late night epiphany:

> . . . it occurred to me
> that *one* night, instead of warm pajamas,
> I'd take off all my clothes
> & cross the damp cold lawn & down the bluff
> into the terrible water & walk forever
> under it out toward the island.

Berryman stated that he was sorry to lose his persona; it is clear that Henry's voice is far better suited to the expression of fears and struggles than is the more impersonal, less consistent mode that dominates most of this final collection.

The five sections, then, with their forty-three poems written in a variety of forms, in a number of voices, about a number of subjects, comprise a curious heterogeneous collection, a gathering together of random pieces, a congeries of notes sent to the world from a soul in a state of extreme agitation, a state that precludes, more often than not, the kind of control required if desperate emotion is to be translated into art. *Delusions, Etc.* lacks the structural coherence that characterizes all of Berryman's other work—especially *Love & Fame*—and it is obvious that the collection was not subjected to the rigorous self-editing and pruning that help give the other works their shape. The book is, in all, an honorable failure, one that raises questions about whether Berryman could have continued to produce had he lived on—though it is altogether possible, each of his books being so remarkably different from the ones that preceded it, that he would have surprised us with a new approach.

One of the stylistic peculiarities that makes this book distinctive, setting it apart in particular from the direct, prosy locutions of *Love & Fame,* is an odd juxtaposition of formal, academic language (relating to canonical hours, Latin phrases, and astronomy,

to give but three examples) with breezy colloquialisms usually associated with adolescence. We encounter on the one hand such
phrases as "in crisis like a skew Wolf-Rayet star," "loafed your
torque," "the poor man in paracme, greeding still," and perhaps
most representative, "Uccello's ark-locked lurid deluge." On the
other hand (the offhand), the poet reverts to "the sweat is,"
"screw that," "I've had it," "some very sharp cookies," and "a
new taste sensation," the latter, since it refers to Eve's apple,
somewhat more tolerable than the others, but operating nevertheless at a cut below the level of cliché. The protagonist of *Recovery* expresses his hatred for such locutions as "hang-ups" and
"up-tight," and this makes Berryman's tolerance for "the sweat is"
etc. all the more puzzling.

This fusing of disparate modes, combining the bookish with the
colloquial, is related to the juxtaposition of language that is odd
and muddled with that characterized by luminous directness and
simplicity. The most effective (and affecting) lines in the book are
those few, clear and deeply felt, that float to the surface from a
murk of clotted rhetoric:

> I'm not a good man
> I am ashamed
> I've got to get as little as possible wrong.
> I still feel rotten about myself
> I have not done well

These spontaneous laments of a man in distress make much of the
surrounding verbiage sound cluttered, cranked out by a nervous,
tinkering imagination. Much of the book's complex religious poetry, in fact, seems to exist at several removes from the poet's
deepest feelings, while the simpler statements emerge because of
emotional necessity. After giving up Henry, Berryman was not

able, consistently, to find a voice that would communicate, believably and consistently, his inner hell, his awful guilt, or his accidie, and the moments in *Delusions, Etc.* that are moving are those most reminiscent of the dream songs. Like so many of the extremist poets, as John Thompson writes, "he found that on the far side of his breakthrough—or his breakdown—everything was flat. Henry, that blithe and desperate spirit, came no longer with his fractured dreamy songs, his soft-shoe shuffle, his baby-talk that frightened the grown-ups with its naked infantilism. Without him, the world was small and orderly like a room made of cement blocks." [2]

The obvious contrasts in the work, between what is mannered and what is deeply felt, go far toward explaining the book's central problem. Berryman is primarily a poet of loss, and when he expresses his griefs, his guilt, his depressions, the language is credible, the poems affecting. In his noisy, disputatious poems, however, one senses that he protests too much, almost as if trying to convince himself, and his God, of his faith, both in individual prayers and in the placement of these prayers at the beginning and end of the book. As A. Alvarez observes, it is as though Berryman were attempting to defend himself against his own depression: "In all truth, it is not the religious note of a genuinely religious man. Berryman's poems to God are his least convincing performances; nervous, insubstantial, mannered to a degree and intensely argumentative." [3] Alvarez (for whom the poet had great respect) holds the view that Berryman's was "a gift for grief," and that his masterpiece is the late *Dream Songs*, in which he mourns a generation of friends and artists, in the process mourning his own impending death. This tone is found in a few of the private poems in the final collection, those in which he had reached "that state of terminal desolation where suicide began to seem to him not merely possible but inevitable." [4] These intensely personal poems—"He Resigns," "No," "Henry by Night," "Henry's Understanding"—make up the radiant center of the book. Next to them the prayers seem strained and somewhat manic—again quoting Alvarez, "Berryman's religious verse seems like a willed, nervous defense against the appalling sadness which permeates the real poems at the heart of the book." [5]

Other critics have responded similarly to the religious poems. Peter Dale claims that Berryman attempted to defend the poems from skepticism by an appearance of doubt, self-mockery, and struggle, and that he banked on a "baffled respect for modernism." (Dale sees in the book "that monstrous egotism and cultural narcissism that are monumental in *The Dream Songs*.") [6] Helen Vendler, calling the book "dead," dismisses the religious poems as "no good." "When he became the redeemed child of God, his shamefaced vocabulary dropped useless, and no poet can be expected to invent, all at once and at the end of his life, a convincing new stance, a new style in architecture along with his change of heart." [7] The play on Auden's "Petition" is witty, but it misses the crucial point that Berryman's redemption, hardly an instant conversion, was a long, tortuous process begun in the *Dream Songs* and continued until his death. *Delusions, Etc.* is a culmination, not a beginning, the changes of heart (and architecture) taking place over many years and through many pages. It is true that the visions "give no new life to his poetry," but the theory of a newly simple heart does not stand up under close scrutiny.

Berryman's friend William Meredith, reviewing the book for *Poetry*, is more gentle, choosing to comment on its strengths and to mention only in passing the troublesome religious poems. He finds at least four major poems in the "new-old unHenry'd voice that he seems to have been rooting around for in the less successful parts of *Love & Fame*," noting particular excellence in "Beethoven Triumphant": "It has the force and complexity of a late quartet or the Great Fugue." [8] A few words on this remarkable poem are clearly in order. Made up of twenty-seven stanzas of from four to eleven lines, the sequence reveals Berryman as historian, music critic, and eulogist. The work is a dramatically personal form of homage, one that bears at times a striking resemblance to *Mistress Bradstreet* in its compressed intensities ("tensing your vision onto an alarm / of gravid measures, sequent to demure"), inclusion of little-known biographical facts ("When brother Johann signed 'Real Estate Owner,' you: 'Brain owner' "), movement from objective narrative to direct address ("Koussevitzky will make it, Master; lie back down"), emphasis on physical decay ("Your body-filth flowed to the middle of the floor"), and introduction of contemporary detail ("I called our chief prose-writer / at home a thousand miles off"). As in *Mistress Bradstreet* Berryman conjures up the spirit of a long dead artist, analyzes, lovingly if somewhat pedantically, the basic qualities of this individual's nature, and provides a kind of valedictory coda. Where the Bradstreet sequence ends on a note of quiet affection, however, this poem closes with a grand crescendo: "You're all over my wall! / You march and chant around here! I hear your thighs." (The final phrase, which sounds curious out of context, actually works, resolving an image introduced in the opening stanza.) These climactic lines are strikingly like the opening of "The Facts & Issues" (section five), in which the poet describes a mystical sense of God's presence: "I really believe He's here all over this room."

Berryman obviously identifies with the composer, whom he shows to be a troubled sleeper, misunderstood, physically disabled, eccentric, churlish, absent-minded, vain. In lines echoing Keats's "Grecian Urn" ode he rejoices in the fact that the man died in his prime, thus spared the burdens of old age: "Ah but the indignities you flew free from, / your self-abasements even would increase." And he attempts to approximate, through his language, the glories of "the B flat major," "the Diabelli varia," and "the 4th Piano Concerto" as a way of documenting this feel-

ing of identification. His long poem is not meant to suggest a concerto, or a sonata, or a symphony, but its richly musical individual lines clearly are attempts to suggest Beethoven's powerful
rhythms and ecstatic tonalities. Nowhere in Berryman is the language purer. The opening lines, for example, melodious, even
cellolike, are representative: "Dooms menace from tumults.
Who's immune / among our mightier of headed men?" In addition to the obvious assonance of Doom-tum(ults)-Who-(im)mune,
there are secondary harmonies provided by from-among-of, and
by men(ace)-head(ed)-men. The slant rhyme (immune-men) and
the numerous "m" sounds add to the consonance, as does the insistent percussive beat. "One chord thrusts, as it must / find al-
lies, foes, resolve, in subdued crescendo," the poet writes later,
the sound once again underscoring the sense of the words. The
poem, despite some regrettable inversions—'Schnabel did
record," "if down he sat"—is a triumphant marriage of form and
meaning.

Given Berryman's admiration for the late flowering he found in
Williams and Yeats as well as in Goya, it is appropriate, even
though his own late work is not for the most part his most brilliant, that this final book should find its noblest moments in a
tribute to Beethoven. It is distressing, nevertheless, that his
"last" book of poems should, as a whole, the National Book
Award nomination notwithstanding, fall so far below the highest
level of the work that preceded it. It is thus somehow fitting that
the other of his major posthumous books should be in prose, and
that it should succeed where many of the final poems fail. *Recovery*, written during the same period as *Delusions, Etc.*, recounts
more memorably than do the poems some of Berryman's struggles, principally to regain the faith of his childhood and to shake
his dependence on alcohol. The novel was left unfinished, an un-
edited typescript and a series of work sheets comprising what was
published. Rough and incomplete as it is, however, it is a strong

and moving work, one of the most important things the poet did, both for its own intrinsic merit and for the light it throws on Berryman and on his poetry, particularly on *The Dream Songs.*

"Our lives had become unmanageable." "We are unregenerate." "I have nothing to lose." "At least he was still alive." These spare sentences document a mood of rock-bottom self-awareness. They also suggest a source of the book's usefulness: *Recovery* consistently makes explicit what in the poetry is frequently ambiguous or implicit. There are numerous passages, particularly those in which the protagonist provides, during therapy, accounts of his chaotic life, that serve as a useful gloss to the poems. Here, for example, is an uninhibited description of the alcohol horrors:

> Relief drinking occasional then constant, increase in alcohol tolerance, first blackouts, surreptitious drinking, growing dependence, urgency of *first* drinks, guilt spreading, unable to bear discussion of the problem, blackout crescendo, failure of ability to stop along with others . . . grandiose and aggressive behaviour, remorse without respite, controls fail, resolutions fail, *decline of other interests* . . . irrational resentments, inability to eat, erosion of the ordinary will, tremor and sweating.
>
> (123–24)

Even more graphic is a long outline-description, read to the therapy group, recounting disreputable events in the protagonist's life. The following details are representative:

> A life centered around whiskey (gin, ale, vodka, rum, brandy) may have byproducts but clearly it is *insane.* The first evidence I remember is 1950, when I gave a public lecture drunk. . . . Three years later my beloved first wife left me after eleven years because of liquor and bad sex. I then drank fifteen hours a day in New York, once *very* seriously planning suicide . . . jumping off the George Washington Bridge cannot fail. . . . Here, the following winter, my

chairman told me one day I had telephoned a girl student at midnight threatening to kill her—no recollection, blacked out. . . . Many injuries drunk, three weeks one mental hospital, half a dozen times another. Four or five incomplete homosexual experiences when drunk. . . . My second wife left me because of liquor and bad sex. . . . Hallucination once. DT's once (six hours). I had an involuntary bowel movement in my clothes.

(170–71)

"The wicked is snared in the work of his own hands" (Psalms 9:16) is the epigraph Berryman selected for this painful book. His chief character, the man whose uncontrolled life is described in the passages above, is Alan Severance, M.D., Litt.D., a Pulitzer Prize winner recently profiled in *Life*. He is supposedly an immunologist and molecular biologist, but his very occasional references to scientific matters and to his own research are the least convincing aspects of the novel. He is obviously a man of letters, referring at one point to an early story, at another to his thirteen published books. His name, if unsubtle, is appropriate, suggesting separation—from God, from his family, from himself, and from "perseverance." His alter ego, Jasper Stone, a bitter bearded poet whose major work is called *The Screams* (and whose name probably comes from *Hero and Leander*), explicates the name: " 'Alan' is *harmony*, right? Celtic, I believe. Your last name is wide open. Tearer-apart of people, disrupter." Severance is immediately reminded of the circle Dante reserves for Sowers-of-Discord. He reciprocates more gently, later, giving the poet a brief critique of his work, clearly based on *The Dream Songs*: "You sound better aloud. Good deal of authentic mania there, black and blue wit, pain—the fellow going on to fresh defeats, flappable, flappable. Surviving, however."

The book, which suggests a journal as much as it does fiction, focuses on the scientist's day by day thoughts, activities, and confessions, sometimes in the first person, sometimes in the third.

There are frequent quotations from his diary. As in most works set in an institution, the book has an airless, antiseptic *No Exit* quality, its characters trapped within the walls of the place, utterly dependent on one another, and on their own resources, for diversion. Unlike what happens in such flamboyant books as *One Flew Over the Cuckoo's Nest* or *A Fan's Notes*, however, the minor characters do not emerge as memorable, lovable eccentrics who manage to make life within the walls seem richer than that outside. Berryman introduces a great many characters, but although some of them come into focus slowly, they remain for the most part an undifferentiated mass of faceless sufferers. The staff members also tend to blur.

The individual personalities of Severance's fellow inmates are less important, however, than is his attitude toward these people. In addition to the epigraph from *Psalms,* the book has another, from Shakespeare: "Oh I have suffered / With those that I saw suffer." Much of the burden of *Recovery* is to show Severance's attempts to get outside himself, away from his own preoccupations, and to identify with the griefs and hopes of his fellow alcoholics. The process is heartbreaking, involving all sorts of small gains and setbacks; it is not possible to read the gently hopeful passages without thinking of the bitterly ironic implications of the title. Removed from all his props and supports, from his brilliant colleagues and admiring students, and from all the things that nurture his delusions (this word appears over and over), Severance is thrown back on himself and forced to discover his long buried humanity. His awards and degrees count for nothing in this democratic world of failures, of housewives and hockey players. In a series of one-to-one encounters and group sessions he is forced to admit certain truths about himself, coming slowly to the point—unless this too is a delusion—of being able to empathize with his badly educated fellow sufferers, and thus to participate in the healing process. In the course of this "recovery" he takes some incredible blows, but somehow manages to survive.

The book is an almost consistently readable (if painfully repetitious) amalgam of conversations, confrontations, anecdotes, flashbacks, and broodings on alcoholism. The latter provide a good
deal of information about Berryman's life, provided one assumes—and all the evidence points to a total identification—that
"Severance" is unambiguously the poet, that the minor and not
altogether convincing disguise is merely a narrative device. The
personal details are useful as a gloss on the poetry—sometimes
specifically, more often generally, providing a sense of some of
the larger events in the poet's life that have contributed to his
present condition.

The "autobiographical" flashbacks are scattered throughout the
book in no discernible pattern. At the risk of imposing too neat
an order on a work that, like *The Dream Songs,* does not move
chronologically, I want to isolate, and in some cases comment on,
some details that help us understand Berryman (and his writing)
somewhat better. To begin with, and this is unusually illuminating, we learn that as an "Eagle Brand baby," one whose
mother could not nurse him, he already had an "insatiable greed
for reassurance." He remembers a few things from his "skimpy
childhood," particularly serving as pallbearer for a friend, whose
dead hand he touches (the source of Song 129), masturbating
with a friend, and seeing his "tall Daddy" splendid in his Sam
Browne belt and saber. He read all of the Oz books, the Tarzan
books, the Tom Swifts and Don Sturdys, and encountered his
first "real story" in Faulkner's "Turn About." He remembers
killing a mocking-bird, being trapped with ripped pants in a tree,
and snuffing candles at Sunday mass. Such is the stuff dreams are
made on.

If "skimpy," these things were also special. But this period of
his life is followed by his father's suicide, by his loss of all personal awareness of God, and by his prep-school years at South
Kent (altered to St. Paul's). Berryman keeps returning to those
years, trying to penetrate the mystery of their emptiness. Early

teens are invariably a time of almost unbearable intensity and of discovery, but for Severance, though he remembers specific events (awe of the old man, butts in the ice-house, erection over Cornelia the matron), there is little to look back on with delight. He regards these years as "the four-year prep-school blackout," "the prep-school oblivion," "an almost-four-year ambition lacuna," and as "his occluded teens." This period, like his lost state of grace, and like his sense of his father, is something he wants desperately to recover.

Berryman/Severance comments on a homosexual encounter during his prep-school years (the one that led to his first suicide attempt), and touches here and there in the book on his doubts about his orientation: "I'm a homosexual, damn you. I just don't do anything about it." There is, though, nothing in Berryman's life or work to suggest anything more than infrequent doubts about his sexual identity. The evidence of his attraction to women, and in particular of his "terrible trouble with young women," is altogether compelling, even though there was a good deal of emotional violence involved in these relationships, and even though compulsive behavior is always suspect. His sexuality was so powerful that at times he envied Origen, who castrated himself, thereby preventing for good the sort of fantasies that Severance finds overwhelming:

> Inappropriate and paralyzing sexual images danced before his closed eyes in their dozens, or hundreds or thousands. Vulvas, hands on him, mouths, hot breasts, spread bottoms, their clenched feet and scissoring, in cemeteries, parks, cars, sand-dunes, darkness and daylight, floors, beds, beds. Heavy breathing, gropings back. Once without even knowing who it was. Friends' wives, virgins. Unspeakable. And the myriad unacted.
>
> (187)

He also has terrible reveries about "female torsos dismembered and strewn," and about "slain nurse's aids strewn around." He is shocked by the sign "Family Butcher" over a shop, his heated imagination giving the harmless phrase literal connotations. Regarding himself as "a monster" and as a "beast" in sex, he shudders with horror remembering that once, drunk, he may have "made a gesture, or said something" to his mother's sister. The worst things he has done in his awful life "were to make three excellent women utterly miserable with my drinking and bad sex and to seduce once after we both married my dearest girl cousin." On another occasion he mentions his illegitimate son, who was nothing but an infant "shitting all over" him nineteen years ago.

We discover the cause of his heavy drinking, the source of virtually all the major problems of his life. "No trouble with liquor before that. What was I—thirty-two. My first adulterous love affair. . . . My mistress drank heavily and I drank along with her, and afterward I just kept on." The reference, of course, is to the "Lise" of the sonnets, who "drank a blue streak." Set in a drying out hospital (Ruth said "Treatment or else"), *Recovery* contains a great many probing analyses of alcoholism and of how it can be handled. Berryman/Severance makes a brave attempt to come to terms with the reasons for his lapses from sobriety. One journal entry in particular is revealing and, in its fusion of self-awareness and delusion, moving:

> Why I slip: 1) False pride ('I am unique': *I* am the one alcoholic who can drink and get away with it.
> 2) Teen-age instability and over-confidence (used to getting away with *anything*, always have done, bec. loved and powerful: *I* can drink and get away with it.
> 3) despair: so why not? (> suicide) I am wicked: and can't bear it sober.
>
> (131)

There are many other entries as well, but this third one is so typical of any compulsive drinker's genius at discovering compelling reasons for his addiction ("Poor me, poor me, pour me a drink") that the additional justifications are redundant.

We get other bits of information about Severance's life and about the sources of his guilt. His first wife, for example, just out of hospital with a slipped disc, announces that she is going to leave him. (A similar scene is described in Eileen Simpson's novel.) His relationship with his son ("I'm scared a lonely. Never see my son," Dream Song 40), whom he has not visited for years ("It was simple: he was an utter bastard"), is analyzed in a painful confrontation that leads to a disturbing epiphany: "But all my priorities are wrong. I see that" (167). He also suffers from his failure to be a proper father to his daughter: "Then when she said to you, 'Daddy never plays with me,' and she cried, my God when I heard that I thought I would die" (37). We also learn several less important things—that "Severance" was "mistreated" by a tyrannical Associate Dean, that his attitude toward fame is ambivalent ("Either I take it too high . . . or I am actually ashamed of it"), that he is an inveterate interrupter, that he is anti-Pope and antagonistic to the Blessed Virgin Mary, and that his only hobby is New Testament criticism.

The most interesting material in the book lies in the protagonist's attempts to discover his true feelings about his parents. Throughout his life (and throughout the *Songs*) Berryman blamed his problems on his father, on the act of betrayal that robbed him of his faith and blotted out his teens. And yet he does not quite know whether to trust his memories. Was he wrong about the "warm close fishing hunting father-duo" he remembered? Was his father, as his mother said, "a *cold* man"? Is it possible that he felt guilt at his father's death, sensing that something he himself had done may have been a cause? Is it conceivable that his present guilt results from his sense of his father's weakness?

'How do I actually now see him: limited, weak, honest (but unfaithful at least twice), prominent only very locally, not a soldier (*fake*

soldier, National Guard)—and do I feel guilty about this rather *con-
temptuous* view, in the face of my real love? Queer that that
Faulkner story hit me so hard, hit me *only,* the sole early work of
art I remember. Very young hero a British torpedo-boat second
officer (my unfailing, planned juniority to somebody), hopeless
drunkard between reckless missions, misunderstood by (older)
American aviators, thought a sissy (me at St. Paul's, because I wore
glasses and didn't go out for football my first year—have always seen
myself ruined there by this, but is it likely? . . .)' The mystery of
what I was reading under the covers after lights-out! Tall handsome
Daddy, adored and lost so soon!

(192)

The most important insight that comes during this period of
self-analysis is the recognition that the major source of his
difficulties may after all be not his dead father but his living
mother. "Have I been wrong all these years, and it was *not*
Daddy's death that blocked my development for so long? Could
this have been a mere separation from Mother?" He speculates
on whether his life-long self-pity may be caused by an "unspeakably powerful possessive adoring MOTHER, whose life at 75 is
still centered wholly on *me*" (80).

And my ('omnipotent') feeling that I can *get away with anything*—
e.g., slips!—has been based on the knowledge that she will *always*
forgive me, always come to the rescue (Fall '53). And my vanity
based on *her* uncritical passionate admiration (letter ten days ago on
my lectures twenty years ago!)—rendering me invulnerable ('indifferent'—a *fact,* too) to all criticism, and impatient with anything
short of total prostration before the products of my genius. . . . My
debts to her immeasurable. . . . *But* she helped destroy my father
and R; affairs w JA, JL, G—others? (>my promiscuity?); horribly
weakened my brother; would never, and *still* hasn't let go of me in
any degree.

(80–81)

His ambivalence to this strong woman is striking. He sees her as
beautiful and courageous, and yet "after a few hours with her I'm

ready to climb the wall. Moreover I feel she's somehow afraid of *me,* God knows why, and that paralyzes me." We are, after all, children all our lives. There is something almost unbearably touching in the spectacle of this middle-aged genius attempting to understand his confused feelings about his mother. It is possible that had these perceptions come earlier she might have replaced "tall handsome Daddy" as the object of the rage and love expressed in the *Songs.*

It is also possible, since Mrs. Berryman was still living, that the poet would have excised or altered some of these passages (even though they are not explicitly autobiographical) had he lived to see the book published. There are things one can say in one's journal, or to one's analyst, that ought not get public exposure, though the portrayal of Lowell's mother and father in *Life Studies* went far toward removing forever the traditional off-limits signs. In any case, it is likely that the work would be decidedly different—firmer, less repetitious, more shapely—had Berryman completed the manuscript. We know from his notes, for example, that a major chapter dealing with his Jewish studies would have rounded out the book.

The notes also show how the novel was to end. Severance would leave the hospital "cured," to the extent of being able to control his unforgivable memory. "The goal of alcoholic treatment, he had really grasped after six months out, was oblivion. . . . He might, certainly, at any time drink again. But it didn't seem likely. He felt calm." The final paragraph was to find him descending Pike's Peak: "He was perfectly ready. No regrets. He was happier than he had ever been in his life before. Lucky, and he didn't deserve it. He was very, very lucky. Bless everybody. He felt—fine."

Notes

INTRODUCTION

1. Elizabeth Nussbaum, "Berryman and Tate: Poets Extraordinaire," *Minnesota Daily*, p. 7.

2. Lewis Hyde, "Alcohol & Poetry: John Berryman and the Booze Talking," *American Poetry Review*, pp. 7–12. "I have shown that the *Dream Songs* can be explicated in terms of the disease of alcoholism. We can hear the booze talking. Its moods are anxiety, guilt, and fear. Its tone is a moan that doesn't resolve. Its themes are unjust pain, resentment, self-pity, pride and a desperate desire to run the world. . . . These poems are not a contribution to culture. They are artifacts of a dying civilization, like one of those loaves of bread turned to lava at Pompeii" (p. 11).

3. John Plotz, et al., "An Interview with John Berryman," *Harvard Advocate*, p. 4.

4. Conversation with Mrs. Berryman, July 11, 1973, at her home in Minneapolis.

5. Jane Howard, "Whisky and Ink, Whisky and Ink," *Life*, p. 76.

6. William Martz, "John Berryman," in *Seven American Poets from MacLeish to Nemerov: An Introduction*, p. 172.

7. "Shirley & Auden" in *Love & Fame*, p. 7. See also "Henry's Fate," *The New York Review of Books*, XXIII:12 (July 15, 1976), p. 28.

8. *Recovery*, p. 68.

9. The sonnets may not be quite so strong as I found them; I was moved not only by the language but by the image of the strong-minded old lady reading (without spectacles) her son's tributes to her as the late afternoon Minneapolis sun warmed her apartment.

10. James Radcliffe Squires, *Allen Tate; A Literary Biography* (New York: Pegasus, 1971), p. 122.

11. Richard Kostelanetz, "Conversation with Berryman," *Massachusetts Review*, p. 342. I am indebted to this essay for details relating to Berryman's education.

12. Elizabeth Nussbaum, "Berryman and Tate," p. 9.

13. *Living Age*, 359 (January 1941), p. 496.

14. "The Loud Hill of Wales," *Kenyon Review*, 2 (Autumn 1940), p. 485. In *The Freedom of the Poet*, p. 285.

15. "More Directions," *Kenyon Review*, 3 (Summer 1941), pp. 386–88.

16. *Canadian Forum*, 22 (October 1942), p. 220.

17. Paul Strachan, *Christian Science Monitor*, October 3, 1942, p. 10.

18. Eileen Simpson, *The Maze* (Simon and Schuster, 1975). Some representative views: "As he pushed to the end of his work on the long poem, his state was becoming alarming. She was beginning to fear for his, always precarious, stability. Night after night now she found him at three and four o'clock asleep in his chair, his fingers burned by the cigarette dangling between them, a ring of burns in the rug beneath his hand" (p. 32). "Hector pulled her hand down. 'You're not going to shut me up. I've been watching you for years. Surprised, aren't you? He's the great man. He makes a mess. You clean up after him. Why? Is the care and feeding of poets so damned interesting? I doubt it. And as for his compulsive sleeping around . . .' " (p. 109). " 'What a strange man Benjamin is! And so changeable! One minute he's a darling, then next minute he's a devil. Isn't it so?' " (p. 141).

19. "The World of Henry James," *Sewanee Review*, 53 (Spring 1945), pp. 291–97.

20. Martz, "John Berryman," pp. 173–74. Mr. Martz does not document his information. According to a note in Linebarger (*John Berryman*, p. 153) the biographical details in Martz's pamphlet were drawn from an interview with Berryman in October 1968.

21. *John Berryman*, p. 157.

22. *Stephen Crane*, p. 25.

23. *The Freedom of the Poet*, p. 140.

24. Alan Seager, *The Glass House* (New York: McGraw-Hill Book Company, 1968), p. 214.

25. In Kostelanetz, "Conversation with Berryman," p. 343.

26. Conversation with Mr. Lars Mazzola, who served as Berryman's teaching assistant while doing graduate work at Minnesota.

27. "Public and Private Poetry," *The Hudson Review*, XXV:2 (Summer 1972), p. 295.

28. *Ibid.*

29. Kostelanetz, "Conversation with Berryman," p. 341.

30. "The Poetry of John Berryman," *New York Review of Books*, May 28, 1964, p. 3.

31. William Heyen, "John Berryman: A Memoir and an Interview," *The Ohio Review*, pp. 46–52. This journal (Winter 1974) features a special section on Ber-

ryman, which includes evaluations by Peter Stitt ("John Berryman: The Dispossessed Poet") and Michael Dennis Browne ("Henry Fermenting: Debts to the Dream Songs"). Since these are thoughtful and affectionate essays, it comes as something of a shock to find, in the same journal, a mean-spirited dismissal of *Recovery* by Louis Simpson (pp. 112–14): "But drunks are boring—there is no exception to this rule—and *Recovery* is about a drunk." Simpson describes Berryman as a man with "a desperate, insatiable desire for fame" whose writing "aims neither at God or man, but only at the media." It is curious that such self-righteous thoughts should emanate from the author of that media book par excellence, *Three on the Tower*, a pastiche of literary anecdotes about Eliot, Pound, and Williams.

32. Donald Davie, "Problems of decorum," *The New York Times Book Review* (April 25, 1976), p. 3. See Robert Giroux's sensitive preface to *The Freedom of the Poet*: "When I saw John, for what was to be the last time, a few weeks later at Sarah's christening, he seemed happier, more confident and serene than in all the years I had known him. . . . He sounded convincing about having licked his drinking problem (he drank only non-alcoholic stuff during my stay in Minneapolis), and was enthusiastic about the progress of his novel, *Recovery*" (p. ix). The most explicit evidence of Berryman's mood in his final days is found in a poem (published in *Henry's Fate*) called "I didn't," written on January 5, 1972, within 48 hours of his suicide: "I didn't. And I didn't. Sharp the Spanish blade / to gash my throat after I'd climbed across / the high railing of the bridge / to tilt out. . . ."

33. Linebarger, *John Berryman*, pp. 22–23.
34. Hyde, "Alcohol & Poetry," p. 12.

CHAPTER 1: THE SHORT POEMS

1. *Living Age*, p. 498.
2. Paul Engle and Joseph Langland, ed., *Poet's Choice* (New York: The Dial Press, 1962), p. 136.
3. "Berryman's 'World's Fair,' " *The Explicator*, 34: 3 (November 1975), Item 22.
4. William Heyen, "John Berryman: A Memoir and an Interview," p. 56.

CHAPTER 2: THE PRINCETON MISTRESS

1. *Berryman's Sonnets* (Farrar, Straus & Giroux, 1967).

CHAPTER 3: A NEW ENGLAND MISTRESS

1. *The Works of Anne Bradstreet*, ed. by Jeannine Hensley (Cambridge, Mass.: Belknap Press of Harvard University Press, 1967), p. xxxiv.
2. "John Berryman," p. 174.

3. "Notes on American Poetry After 1945," *The American Review*, 1 (Autumn 1960), pp. 127–35. "He bided his time," Fitzgerald wrote, "and made the poem of his generation."

4. Jacket blurb for *Homage to Mistress Bradstreet and Other Poems* (Farrar, Straus & Giroux, 1968).

5. Holmes: "Speaking in Verse," *New York Times Book Review* (September 30, 1956), p. 18. Flint: "A Romantic on Early New England," *New Republic* (May 27, 1957), p. 28.

6. Aiken, Lowell, and Kunitz quotations all from Kunitz, "No Middle Flight," *Poetry*, 90 (July 1957), pp. 244–49.

7. "The Researched Mistress," *Saturday Review*, 4:36 (March 23, 1957), pp. 36–37.

8. *The New Yorker*, 33:111 (March 2, 1957), p. 33.

9. "One Answer to a Question: Changes," in *The Freedom of the Poet*, p. 328.

10. *Ibid.*, p. 329.

11. After writing the first stanza and three lines of the second Berryman remained "stuck" for nearly five years. He "accumulated details and sketched, fleshing out the target or vehicle, still under the impression that seven or eight stanzas would see it done. There are fifty-seven. My stupidity is traceable partly to an astuteness that made me as afraid as the next man of the ferocious commitment involved in a long poem and partly to the fact that although I had my form and subject, I did not have my theme yet. This emerged, and under the triple impetus of events I won't identify, I got the poem off the ground and nearly died following it." (*The Freedom of the Poet*, p. 328.)

12. Dorothy Strudwick, "Homage to Mr. Berryman," *Minnesota Daily* (November 5, 1956), p. 6.

13. *The Freedom of the Poet*, p. 328.

14. *Ibid.* See also "Homage to Mr. Berryman," p. 6.

15. For a full and intelligent analysis of the relationship between the poem and Bradstreet's work, see Alan Holder, "Anne Bradstreet Resurrected," *Concerning Poetry*, 2 (Spring 1969), pp. 11–18.

16. *American Poets from the Puritans to the Present* (Dell Publishing Company, 1968), p. 8.

CHAPTER 4: THE LONELY
LAMENTS OF HENRY PUSSYCAT

1. *Recovery* (Farrar, Straus & Giroux, 1974), p. xiv. The foreward, Louis Simpson writes in his vicious review (see note 32, Introduction), "is better fiction than anything in the book." "On Berryman's *Recovery*," *The Ohio Review*, p. 113.

2. All quotations are from *The Dream Songs* (Farrar, Straus & Giroux). I am grateful to a very remarkable former student, David Ogden, for suggesting the pattern of anatomical references.

3. "In Loving Memory of the Late Author of 'The Dream Songs,' " in *John Berryman: a Checklist,* ed. Richard J. Kelly, p. xiii.

4. Paul Wardzinski, while a student of Robert Regan at the University of Pennsylvania, discovered that "Henry House or Charles Henry House was a member of the House family memorialized by Julia A. Moore (1847–1920) in a number of poems."

> God has took their little treasure,
> And his name I'll tell you now.
> He has gone from each forever
>   Their little Charles Henry House.

"Little Henry" in *The Sentimental Song Book* (Cleveland: Ryder Publishing Company, 1877). "Berryman's *The Dream Songs,*" *The Explicator,* 34:9 (May 1976), Item 70.

5. "In a classroom," Donald Hall writes, "the first and longest standing enemies to the teaching of poetry are these notions, common among students, and obviously among many teachers: 1) that poems are *problems* which have *answers;* 2) that there is *a meaning,* which corresponds—in this barbaric esthetic and psychology—to 'what the poet was trying to say': some doctrine of intentions accompanied by the poet's riddle-making perversity, or by her [sic] incompetence of expression; 3) that there is always, somehow, an answer in the back of the book or in the teacher's manual, if only somebody will stop being coy and reveal it." "Knock Knock," *The American Poetry Review,* 5:3, 1976, p. 17.

6. *Recovery,* p. x.

7. *John Berryman: a Checklist,* p. viii.

8. I am deeply indebted to Berryman's close friend Dr. Boyd Thomes for this information. Any readings that were suggested (or reinforced) by Dr. Thomes during two memorable evenings of going through the *Songs* together will be indicated in notes.

9. *Ibid.*

10. *Ibid.*

11. *Crowell's Handbook of Contemporary American Poetry,* 1973, p. 32.

12. Dr. Thomes pointed up the unusual importance of this poem.

13. Tadeusz Borowski, *This Way for the Gas, Ladies and Gentlemen* (New York: The Viking Press, 1959). ("The Supper," pp. 132–36.)

14. Jeffrey Bottiger suggested this reading to me. The point is also made by Ernest Stefanik in "Knowing Henry: A Reading of Dream Song 1" in *John Berryman Studies,* 1:4 (Fall 1975), p. 28. I read the issue of this journal devoted to the song after writing my own analysis, and picked up several new insights. Richard Kelly, for example, relates the tree to the "flashing & bursting tree" of Song 75, and also links the song to number 328, in which Henry "flourish like a sycamore tree" (p. 10). Jo Brans points out that the sycamore, according to Frazer, is traditionally as-

sociated with the rites of Spring: "Presumably the narrator's song was the lyrical perfection of poetry in Eden. Times have changed, the clear daylight time has yielded to night, and the Dream Songs that were to come emerge from a disintegrated personality" (p. 14).

15. I gave the second character a name as a matter of convenience, and choose "Tambo" on the basis of Carl Wittke's *Tambo and Bones, A History of the American Minstrel Stage* (Durham, North Carolina: Duke University Press, 1930). This book is the source of Berryman's first epigraph, " 'GO IN, BRACK MAN, DE DAY'S YO' OWN.' "

16. Dr. Thomes suggested this reading.

17. Berryman sent this poem to Dr. Thomes on April 5, 1958, with the message, "You understand; this is (not me, but) Henry, the—hero?—of my next poem, begun in 1955 & *nowhere*."

18. Recording of the National Poetry Festival, held in Coolidge Auditorium, October 22–24, 1962.

19. Kelly, *John Berryman: a Checklist,* p. xii.

20. Howard, "Whisky and Ink," p. 76.

21. *Ibid.*

22. See note 2, Introduction.

23. Kostelanetz, "Conversation with Berryman," p. 346.

24. *Ibid.*, pp. 344–45.

25. *"Song of Myself:* Intention and Substance," in *The Freedom of the Poet,* p. 230.

CHAPTER 5: AFTER THE SONGS

1. "The Art of Poetry XVI," *The Paris Review* (Winter 1972), p. 179.

2. *Ibid.*, p. 200.

3. *Ibid.*, p. 201.

4. "John Berryman: A Question of Imperial Sway," in *Contemporary Poetry in America,* ed. Robert Boyers (New York: Schocken Books, 1974), p. 69.

5. "The Art of Poetry XVI," p. 201.

6. *Ibid.*

7. *Ibid.*

8. Foreward to *Recovery,* p. xiii.

9. "Hopkins with no audience and Bridges with thirty readers. He says 'Fame in itself is nothing. The only thing that matters is virtue. Jesus Christ is the only true literary critic.' " "The Art of Poetry XVI," p. 180.

10. *Ibid.*, p. 202.

11. *Ibid.*, pp. 203–4.

12. Howard, "Whisky and Ink," p. 70.

13. "On Berryman's *Recovery,*" p. 112.

14. Carbondale and Edwardsville: Southern Illinois University Press, 1973.

15. *Ibid.*, p. 97.
16. *Ibid.*, p. 104.
17. "John Berryman: A Memoir and an Interview," p. 48.

CHAPTER 6: ISLANDS OF SUFFERING: THE LAST BOOKS

1. "Problems of decorum," p. 4.
2. "Last Testament," *The New York Review of Books* (April 9, 1973), p. 4.
3. *The New York Times Book Review* (June 25, 1972), p. 1.
4. *Ibid.*
5. *Ibid.*
6. "Three Poets: Can Belief and Form Come in Bags of Tricks?" *Saturday Review of Literature*, 55:57 (July 9, 1972), p. 58.
7. *Yale Review*, 62:412 (March 1973), p. 425.
8. "Swan Songs," *Poetry*, 122:2 (May 1973), p. 101.

Bibliography

I. BY JOHN BERRYMAN

Berryman's Sonnets. New York: Farrar, Straus & Giroux, 1967.

Stephen Crane. New York: William Sloan Associates, 1950.

Delusions, Etc. New York: Farrar, Straus & Giroux, 1972.

The Dispossessed. New York: William Sloan Associates, 1948.

The Dream Songs. New York: Farrar, Straus & Giroux, 1969. (Contains 77 *Dream Songs*, 1964, and *His Toy, His Dream, His Rest,* 1968.)

"Five New Poems." *American Poetry Review*, 5:4 (1976), pp. 4–5.

Henry's Fate & Other Poems, 1967–1972. New York: Farrar, Straus & Giroux, 1977.

The Freedom of the Poet. New York: Farrar, Straus & Giroux, 1976.

His Thought Made Pockets & the Plane Buckt. Pawlet, Vermont: C. Fredericks, 1958.

Homage to Mistress Bradstreet. New York: Farrar, Straus & Giroux, 1956.

Homage to Mistress Bradstreet and Other Poems. New York: Farrar, Straus & Giroux, 1970.

Love & Fame. New York: Farrar, Straus & Giroux, 1970. (Second edition, revised, 1972.)

"MPLS, MOTHER," *Minneapolis Tribune* (December 1, 1974), ID.

"Our Sins Are More Than We Can Bear" (story), *Twin Cities Express*, (October 1, 1973), p. 19.

Poems. Norfolk, Conn.: New Directions, 1942.

"Posthumous Dream Songs," *The New Yorker* (May 19, 1975), p. 44.
Recovery. New York: Farrar, Straus & Giroux, 1973.
Short Poems. New York: Farrar, Straus & Giroux, 1967.
"Twenty Poems," *Five Young American Poets.* Norfolk Conn.: New Directions, 1940.
"Two Poems," *The Atlantic Monthly,* 236:5 (November 1975), pp. 68–69.
"Unpublished Poems from the Hospital: A Special APR Supplement," *The American Poetry Review,* 4:1 (1975), pp. 17–24.

Editions

Dreiser, Theodore. *The Titan.* Afterword by John Berryman. New York: New American Library, 1965.
Lewis, Matthew G. *The Monk.* Ed. Louis F. Peck. Introduction by John Berryman. New York: Grove Press, 1952.
Nashe, Thomas. *The Unfortunate Traveller, or, The Life of Jack Wilson.* Ed. with an introduction by John Berryman. New York: C. P. Putnam, 1960.

II. BY OTHERS

Alvarez, A[lfred]. *Beyond All This Fiddle.* London: Penguin, 1968.
—— Review of *Delusions, Etc.,* in *The New York Times Book Review* (June 25, 1972), 1.
—— *The Savage God: A Study of Suicide.* New York: Random House, 1972, *passim.*
Bayley, John. "John Berryman: a Question of Imperial Sway," in *Contemporary Poetry in America,* ed. Robert Boyers. New York: Schocken Books, 1974, pp. 59–77.
John Berryman Studies, ed. Ernest Stefanik, Derry, Pa., a quarterly devoted to research-based articles and essays on Berryman and other middle-generation American poets. Vol. 1, No. 1 appeared in January 1975.
Blum, Morgan. "Berryman as Biographer, Stephen Crane as Poet," *Poetry,* 78 (August 1951), 298–307.
Browne, Michael Dennis. "Henry Fermenting: Debts to the *Dream Songs,*" *The Ohio Review,* 15:2 (Winter 1974), 75–87.
Carruth, Hayden. "Love, Art, and Money," *The Nation,* 211 (November 2, 1970), 437–38.
Ciardi, John. "The Researched Mistress," *Saturday Review* (March 23, 1957), 36–37.

Connelly, Kenneth. "Henry Pussycat, He Come Home Good," *Yale Review*, 58 (Spring 1969), 419–27.

Cott, Jonathan. "Theodore Roethke and John Berryman: Two Dream Poets," in Richard Kostelanetz, ed., *On Contemporary Literature.* New York: Avon Books, 1964, 520–31.

Davie, Donald. "Problems of decorum" (review of *Recovery*), *The New York Times Book Review* (April 25, 1976), 3–4.

Dodsworth, Martin. "John Berryman: An Introduction," in *The Survival of Poetry.* London: Faber and Faber, 1970, pp. 100–32.

Donoghue, Denis. "Berryman's Long Dream," *Art International* (March 20, 1969), 61–64.

Dunn, Douglas. "Gaiety & Lamentation: The Defeat of John Berryman," *Encounter*, 43 (August 1974), 72–77.

Eckman, Frederick. "Moody's Ode: The Collapse of the Heroic," *University of Texas Studies in English*, 36 (1957), Annual, 80–92.

Flint, R. W. "A Romantic on Early New England," *New Republic* (May 27, 1957), 28.

Galassi, Jonathan. "John Berryman: Sorrows and Passions of His Majesty the Ego," *Poetry Nation*, 2 (1974), 117–24.

Hamilton, Ian. "John Berryman," *London Magazine*, 4 (February 1965), 93–100.

Heyen, William. "John Berryman: A Memoir and an Interview," *The Ohio Review*, 15:2 (Winter 1974), 46–65.

Hoffman, Daniel. "John Berryman" in *Contemporary Poets of the English Language*, Rosalie Murphy, ed. Chicago: St. James Press, 1970, pp. 85–87.

Holder, Alan. "Anne Bradstreet Resurrected," *Concerning Poetry* (Western Washington State College), 2 (Spring 1969), 11–18.

Howard, Jane. "Whisky and Ink, Whisky and Ink," *Life*, LXIII (July 21, 1967), 67–76.

Hughes, Daniel. "John Berryman and the Poet's Pardon," *American Poetry Review*, II (July-August 1973), 19–22.

Hyde, Lewis. "Alcohol & Poetry: John Berryman and The Booze Talking," *American Poetry Review*, 4:4 (1975), 7–12.

Jarrell, Randall. "Verse Chronicle," *The Nation* (July 17, 1948), 80–81.

Johnson, Carol. "John Berryman and Mistress Bradstreet: A Relation of Reason," *Essays in Criticism*, 14 (October 1964), 388–96.

Kalstone, David. Review of *Recovery*, in *The New York Times Book Review* (May 27, 1973), 1.

Kelly, Richard J. *John Berryman: a Checklist*. Metuchen, N.J.: The Scarecrow Press, 1972.

Kostelanetz, Richard. "Conversation with Berryman," *Massachusetts Review*, 11 (Spring 1970), 34–47.

(Anonymous). "The Life of the Modern Poet" (review of *Delusions, Etc.*), *The Times Literary Supplement* (February 23, 1973), 1–3.

Linebarger, J. M. *John Berryman*. New York: Twayne Publishers, Inc., 1974.

Lowell, Robert. "The Poetry of John Berryman," *New York Review of Books* (May 28, 1964), 2–3.

McBride, Margaret M. "Berryman's 'World's Fair,' " *The Explicator*, 34:3 (November 1975), Item 22.

Malkoff, Karl. *Crowell's Handbook of Contemporary American Poetry*. New York: Thomas Y. Crowell Company, 1973.

Martz, William J. *John Berryman*. Minneapolis: University of Minnesota Press, 1969. In *Seven American Poets from MacLeish to Nemerov: An Introduction*, ed. Denis Donoghue. Minneapolis: University of Minnesota Press, 1975, pp. 171–208.

Mendelson, Edward. "How to Read Berryman's *Dream Songs*," in *American Poetry Since 1960—Some Critical Perspectives*, ed. Robert B. Shaw. Chester Springs, Pa.: Dufour Eds., 1974.

Meredith, William. "Henry Tasting All the Secret Bits of Life: Berryman's Dream Songs," *Wisconsin Studies in Contemporary Literature*, 6 (Winter-Spring 1965), 27–33.

—— "A Bright Surviving Actual Scene: Berryman's 'Sonnets,' " *Harvard Advocate*, 103 (Spring 1969), 19–22.

Mills, Ralph J., Jr. *Creation's Very Self: On the Personal Element in Recent American Poetry*. Fort Worth: Texas Christian University Press, 1969, *passim*.

Neill, Edward. "Ambivalence of Berryman: An Interim Report," *Critical Quarterly*, XVI (Fall 1974), 267–76.

Nims, John Frederick, "Homage in Measure to Mr. Berryman," *Prairie Schooner*, 32 (Spring 1958), 1–7.

Nussbaum, Elizabeth. "Berryman and Tate: Poets Extraordinaire," *Minnesota Daily* (November 9, 1967), 7–10.

Oberg, Arthur. "John Berryman: *The Dream Songs* and the Horror of Unlove," *University of Windsor Review*, 6 (Fall 1970), 1–11.

Phillips, Robert. *The Confessional Poets*. Carbondale: Southern Illinois University Press, 1973.

Porterfield, J. R. "The Melding of a Man: Berryman, Henry, and the Ornery Mr. Bones," *Southwest Review*, LVIII (Winter 1973), 30–46.

Rosenthal, M. L. *The New Poets: American and British Poetry Since World War II*. New York: Oxford University Press, 1967.

Seidel, Frederick. "Berryman's Dream Songs," *Poetry*, 105 (January 1965), 257–59.

Simpson, Eileen. *The Maze*. New York: Simon and Schuster, 1975.

Simpson, Louis. "On Berryman's *Recovery*," *The Ohio Review*, 15:2 (Winter 1974), 112–14.

Sisson, Jonathan. "My Whiskers Fly: An Interview with John Berryman," *Ivory Tower*, XIV (October 3, 1966), 14–18.

Stefanik, Ernest C. "A Cursing Glory: John Berryman's *Love & Fame*," *Renascence*, 25:3 (Spring 1973), 115–27.

—— *John Berryman: A Descriptive Bibliography*. Pittsburgh: University of Pittsburgh Press, 1974.

Stitt, Peter A. "The Art of Poetry XVI," *The Paris Review*, 14 (Winter 1972), 117–207. Interview with Berryman.

—— "John Berryman: The Dispossessed Poet," *The Ohio Review*, 15:2 (Winter 1974), 66–74.

Strudwick, Dorothy. "Homage to Mr. Berryman," *Minnesota Daily* (November 5, 1956), 6.

Thompson, John. "Last Testament" (review of *Delusions, Etc.*), *New York Review of Books* (August 9, 1973), 3–6.

Van Doren, Mark. *Autobiography*. New York: Harcourt, Brace and Co., 1968, pp. 211–13.

Vendler, Helen. "Savage, Rueful, Irrepressible Henry," *New York Times Book Review* (November 3, 1968), 1.

Index